D0962367

Wings Of Song

UNITY BOOKS
Unity Village, Missouri

ACKNOWLEDGMENTS

The publishers wish to express appreciation to James Dillet Freeman, Vice-President of Unity School of Christianity and former director of Silent Unity, for perceiving the need for this hymnbook and for providing the impetus that enabled it to become a reality.

We are grateful to the Association of Unity Churches hymnbook committee: Marilyn Rieger, chairman; Janet Bowser Manning; Warren Meyer; Barbara Provost; Alan Stanley; Harold Whaley; and Viola Williamson for countless hours of valuable time and consideration in selecting the contents.

Thanks go to authors, composers, and publishing companies for granting permission for use of their copyrighted materials, and to Lau's Music Engraving Company for its fine work.

Our gratitude goes to Thomas E. Witherspoon, former editor of Unity Books, and Pamela Yearsley, editor of Unity Books, for counsel, editing, proofreading, and for guiding the publication process.

We especially wish to recognize the outstanding contribution of Sharon Patterson, music editor, for her musical expertise and dedication to detail in research, transposition, manuscript preparation, and liaison with publishers and engravers.

A diligent search has been made to establish the status of all material included. Every effort was made to locate and contact all owners and copyright holders of the enclosed material. If any omissions or errors have been made, we hope they will be brought to our attention immediately so that proper acknowledgment can be made in the future.

Unity School of Christianity

Cover design by
Belinda Newill

Wings
Of
Song

Praise God That Good Is Everywhere   1

OLD 100th
Genevan Psalter
Attr. to Louis Bourgeois

Murray

Praise God that good is ev - ery - where; Praise
to the love we all may share, The life that thrills in
you and me; Praise to the Truth that sets us free.

2

The Lord's Prayer

MALOTTE
Albert Hay Malotte
Arranged by Fred Bock

Matthew 6:9–13

Our Fa-ther, who art in heav-en, hal-low-ed
be Thy name. Thy king-dom come,
Thy will be done on earth as it is in
heav - en. Give us this day our dai - ly

3 Let There Be Peace on Earth

Jill Jackson

PEACE SONG
Sy Miller

4   Holy, Holy, Holy, Lord God Almighty

Adapted from Reginald Heber

NICAEA
John B. Dykes

1. Ho-ly, ho-ly, ho - ly! Lord God Al - might - y!
2. Ho-ly, ho-ly, ho - ly! All the saints a - dore Thee,
3. Ho-ly, ho-ly, ho - ly! Though the dark-ness hide Thee,
4. Ho-ly, ho-ly, ho - ly! Lord God Al - might - y!

Ear - ly in the morn - ing our song shall rise to Thee;
Cast - ing down their gold - en crowns a - round the glass -y sea;
Though the err - ing eye of man Thy glo - ry may not see,
All Thy works shall praise Thy name in earth and sky and sea;

Ho-ly, ho-ly, ho - ly, mer - ci - ful and might - y!
Cher-u -bim and ser-a-phim fall - ing down be - fore Thee,
On-ly Thou art ho - ly, there is none be - side Thee,
Ho-ly, ho-ly, ho - ly, mer - ci - ful and might - y!

Which wert, and art, and ev - er-more shalt be.
Which wert, and art, and ev - er-more shalt be.
Per - fect in power, in love, and pur - i - ty.
Which wert, and art, and ev - er-more shalt be.

From All That Dwell Below the Skies

5

Stanzas 1, 2, Isaac Watts
Stanza 3, Anonymous

DUKE STREET
John Hatton

1. From all that dwell be - low the skies,
2. E - ter - nal are Thy mer - cies, Lord;
3. In ev - ery land be - gin the song;

Let the Cre - a - tor's praise a - rise;
E - ter - nal Truth at - tends Thy word;
To ev - ery land the strains be - long;

Let the Re - deem - er's name be sung,
Thy praise shall sound from shore to shore,
In cheer - ful sounds all voic - es raise,

Through ev - ery land, by ev - ery tongue.
Till suns shall rise and set no more.
And fill the world with loud - est praise.

6 Morning Has Broken

BUNESSAN
Gaelic Melody
Harmonized by David Evans, 1874–1948

Eleanor Farjeon

1. Morn-ing has bro - ken Like the first morn - ing, Black-bird has spo - ken Like the first bird. Praise for the sing - ing!
2. Sweet the rain's new fall Sun - lit from heav - en, Like the first dew - fall On the first grass. Praise for the sweet - ness
3. Mine is the sun - light! Mine is the morn - ing Born of the one light E - den saw play! Praise with e - la - tion,

Words from "The Children's Bells," Oxford University Press.
Used by permission of David Higham Associates Ltd., London.
Music from the "Revised Church Hymnary 1927" by permission of Oxford University Press.

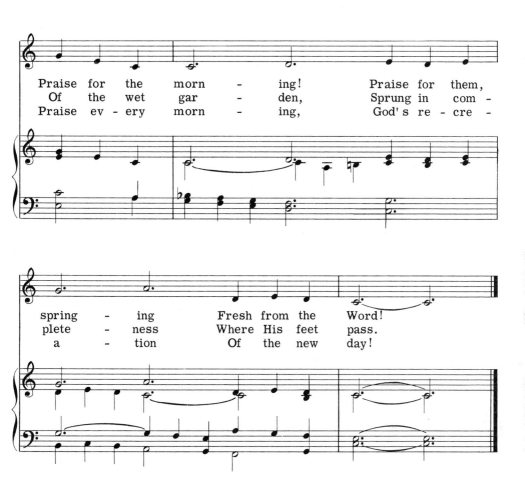

Praise for the morn - ing! Praise for them,
Of the wet gar - den, Sprung in com -
Praise ev - ery morn - ing, God's re - cre -

spring - ing Fresh from the Word!
plete - ness Where His feet pass.
a - tion Of the new day!

7 God Will Take Care

MARTIN
W. Stillman Martin

Civilla D. Martin

1. All I may need He will pro-vide, God will take care of me;
2. Be not dis-mayed what-e'er be-tide, God will take care of you;
3. No mat-ter what may be the test, God will take care of us;

Noth-ing I ask will be de-nied, God will take care of me.
Be-neath His wings of love a-bide, God will take care of you.
Lean, trust-ing one, up-on His breast, God will take care of us.

Refrain

me,
God will take care of you, Through ev-ery day, o'er all the way;
us,

me,
He will take care of you, God will take care of you.
us, us.

We Praise Thee, O God

Stanzas 1 and 2, adapted from Wm. P. Mackay
Stanzas 3 and 4, Anonymous

REVIVE US AGAIN
John J. Husband

1. We praise Thee, O God, For the Spir - it of light, That has shown us Thy good - ness And scat - tered our night.
2. All glo - ry and praise, For Thy like - ness with - in; As the sons of the Fa - ther, Our tri - umphs be - gin.
3. Re - joice and re - joice! Let the Son in you shine; Give praise and thanks - giv - ing For love that's di - vine.
4. Re - joice and be glad For the life of to - day; And the prom - ise it car - ries: "I'm with you al - way."

Refrain

Hal - le - lu - jah! Thine the glo - ry; Hal - le - lu - jah! a - gain!

Hal - le - lu - jah! Thine the glo - ry; We praise Thee, A - men.

9 God of the Earth, the Sky, the Sea

ST. CATHERINE

Samuel Longfellow
Refrain, Anonymous

Henri F. Hemy
Adapted by James G. Walton

1. God of the earth, the sky, the sea,
2. Thy love is in the sun - shine's glow,

Mak - er of all a - bove, be - low, Cre - a - tion
Thy life is in the quick - ening air; When light-nings

lives and moves in Thee. Thy pres - ent life through
flash and storm winds blow, There is Thy power; Thy

Refrain

all doth flow.
law is there.

We give Thee thanks, Thy name we

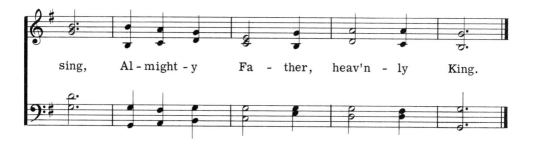

sing, Al - might - y Fa - ther, heav'n - ly King.

Bless the Lord, O My Soul

10

Ippolitov-Ivanov

Bless the Lord, O my soul,

Bless-ed art Thou, O Lord.

11   Oh! That Is Now Glory for Me

Myrtle Fillmore
Refrain adapted from Charles H. Gabriel

GLORY SONG
Charles H. Gabriel

1. Ban-ished all bur-dens of sor-row and pain,
2. Life, like a riv-er of in-fi-nite grace,

My soul's a-glow with an in-fi-nite flame;
Mir-rors the light of His glo-ri-ous face,

My voice, ex-ult-ant, now sings this re-frain,
Mak-ing of Earth a most heav-en-ly place

An-them of glo-ry, oh, glo-ry for me.
Filled with His pres-ence, oh, glo-ry for me!

12 Let All the World in Every Corner Sing

ALL THE WORLD

George Herbert

Robert G. McCutchan

1. Let all the world in ev-ery cor-ner sing: My God and King!
2. Let all the world in ev-ery cor-ner sing: My God and King!

The heavens are not too high, His praise may thith-er fly; The
The church with psalms must shout, No door can keep them out; But,

earth is not too low, His prais-es there may grow. Let
more than all, the heart Must bear the long-est part. Let

all the world in ev-ery cor-ner sing: My God and King!
all the world in ev-ery cor-ner sing: My God and King!

All Hail the Power

13

CORONATION
Oliver Holden

Henry Victor Morgan

14 All Things Bright and Beautiful

ROYAL OAK
17th Century English Melody
Harmonization by V. Earle Copes

Cecil Frances Alexander

All things bright and beau - ti - ful, All crea-tures great and small, All things wise and won - der - ful: The Lord God made them all.

1. Each lit - tle flower that o - pens, Each
2. The pur - ple - head - ed moun - tain, The
3. The cold wind in the win - ter, The
4. He gave us eyes to see them, And

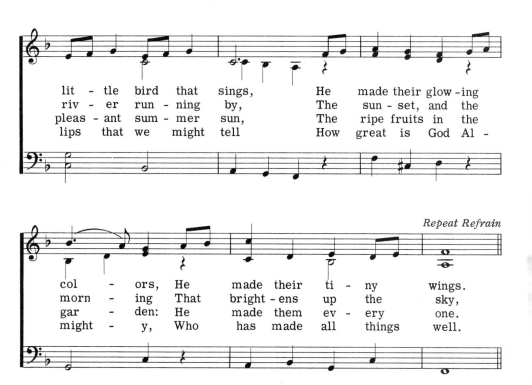

Repeat Refrain

lit - tle	bird	that	sings,	He	made their glow -ing
riv - er	run - ning	by,	The	sun - set, and the
pleas - ant	sum - mer	sun,	The	ripe fruits in the
lips	that we	might	tell	How	great is God Al -

col - ors,	He	made their	ti - ny	wings.
morn - ing	That	bright - ens	up the	sky,
gar - den:	He	made them	ev - ery	one.
might - y,	Who	has made	all things	well.

Alleluia! Amen 15

From a Trad. Hungarian Melody

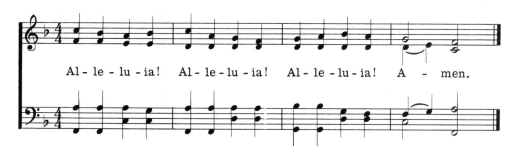

Al - le - lu - ia! Al - le - lu - ia! Al - le - lu - ia! A - men.

16   Amazing Grace

AMAZING GRACE
Early American Melody
Harmonized by Edwin O. Excell

Adapted from John Newton

1. A - maz - ing grace, how sweet the sound That
2. 'Twas grace that taught my heart to sing, And
3. Through man - y dan - gers, toils, and snares I

saved a soul like me! I
grace my fears re - lieved; How
have al - read - y passed; 'Tis

once was lost, but now am found, Was
pre - cious did that grace ap - pear The
grace that brought me safe thus far, To

blind, but now I see.
hour I first be - lieved!
free - dom that will last.

* An optional fourth verse may be the repetition of the words "Praise God!" to the melody.

Our Father, God, to Thee

17

AMERICA
Anonymous

Anonymous

1. Our Fa - ther, God, to Thee, Through - out e - ter - ni - ty, Thy name we praise! Thou art the source of all; Thou lov - est great and small; Thy life sus - tain - eth all; Thine be the praise!

2. I am Thy child of health; I am Thine heir of wealth; All Thine is mine. Joy and pros - per - i - ty Are ev - er mine in Thee, Wis - dom and har - mo - ny And love di - vine.

18   All Creatures of Our God and King

LASST UNS ERFREUEN

St. Francis of Assisi
Tr. by William H. Draper, 1855-1933

Melody from *Geistliche Kirchengesänge,* 1623
Arr. by Ralph Vaughan Williams, 1872-1958

Unison

1. All   crea-tures of   our God   and   King,   Lift
2. Thou   rush - ing wind that art   so   strong,   Ye
3. Thou   flow - ing wa - ter, pure and   clear,   Make
4. And   all   ye men of ten - der   heart,   For -
5. Let   all   things their cre - a - tor   bless,   And

up   your voice and with   us   sing   Al - le -
clouds that sail in heaven a -   long,   O
mu - sic for   thy Lord to   hear,   Al - le -
giv - ing oth - ers, take your   part,   O
wor - ship Him   in hum - ble - ness,   O

lu   -   ia!   Al - le - lu - ia!   Thou
praise   Him!   Al - le - lu - ia!   Thou
lu   -   ia!   Al - le - lu - ia!   Thou
sing   ye!   Al - le - lu - ia!   Ye
praise   Him!   Al - le - lu - ia!   Praise,

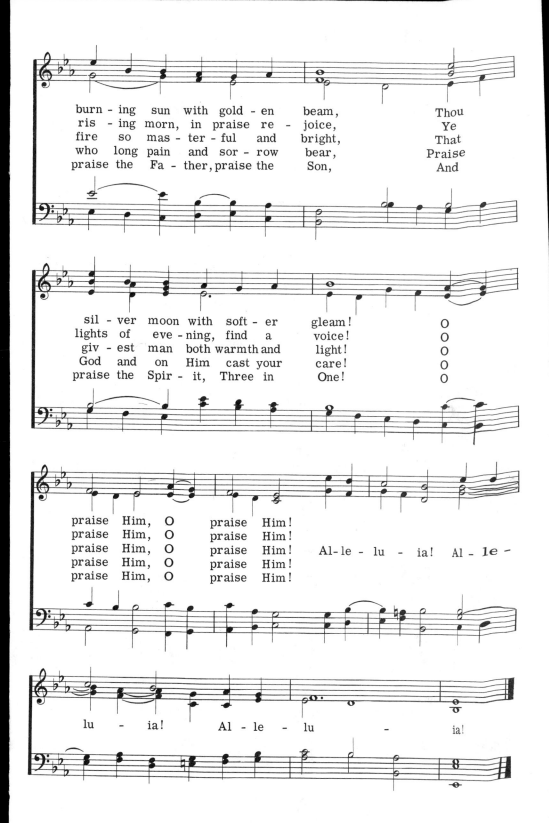

burn - ing sun with gold - en beam, Thou
ris - ing morn, in praise re - joice, Ye
fire so mas - ter - ful and bright, That
who long pain and sor - row bear, Praise
praise the Fa - ther, praise the Son, And

sil - ver moon with soft - er gleam! O
lights of eve - ning, find a voice! O
giv - est man both warmth and light! O
God and on Him cast your care! O
praise the Spir - it, Three in One! O

praise Him, O praise Him!
praise Him, O praise Him!
praise Him, O praise Him! Al - le - lu - ia! Al - le -
praise Him, O praise Him!
praise Him, O praise Him!

lu - ia! Al - le - lu - ia!

19

Rejoice Today with One Accord

EIN' FESTE BURG

Melody by Martin Luther

Adapted from Henry W. Baker

1. Re - joice to - day with one ac - cord, Sing out with ex - ul -
2. Re - joice to - day with words of power, Sing of His love a -

ta - tion; U - nite and praise the might-y Lord With
bid - ing; O trust in God what - e'er the hour, His

joy -ful dec- la - ra - tion; His works of love pro - claim The
love is all-pro - vid - ing. Tri - um-phant songs of praise To

great-ness of His name; For He is God a - lone, Who
Him our hearts shall raise; Now ev - ery voice shall say, "O

21   There Is Sunshine in My Soul Today

SUNSHINE
John R. Sweney

Adapted from Eliza E. Hewitt

1. There is sun - shine in my soul to - day,
2. There is spring - time in my soul to - day.
3. There is glad - ness in my soul to - day,

It is glo - ri - ous and bright,
I know the Lord is near;
And hope, and love, and praise,

Ev - er glow - ing with a warm - ing ray
The notes of peace sing in my heart,
For bless - ings which He gives me now,

For Je - sus is my light.
The joys of grace ap - pear.
Are bright - 'ning all my days.

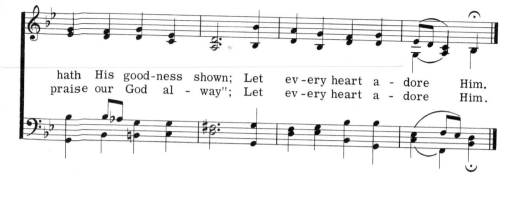

hath His good-ness shown; Let ev-ery heart a - dore Him.
praise our God al - way"; Let ev-ery heart a - dore Him.

Introit

20

Mildred Raymer

Mildred Raymer

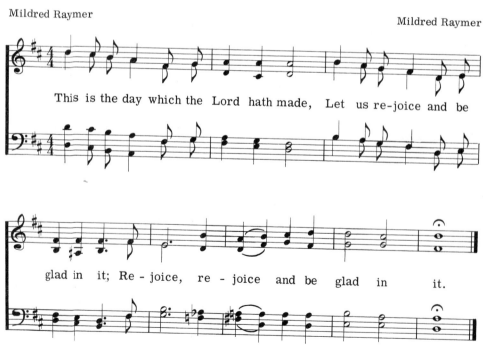

This is the day which the Lord hath made, Let us re-joice and be

glad in it; Re - joice, re - joice and be glad in it.

22   O Worship the King

LYONS

Adapted from Robert Grant   Adapted from J. Michael Haydn

1. O wor-ship the King, all glo-rious a - bove, And
2. Thy boun - ti - ful care, what tongue can re - cite? It
3. Our Fa - ther and God, how faith - ful Thy love! While

grate - ful - ly sing His won - der - ful love; Our
breathes in the air, it shines in the light; It
an - gels de - light to hymn Thee a - bove, The

shield and de - fend - er, the An - cient of Days, Pa -
streams from the hills, it de - scends to the plain, And
hu - man cre - a - tion, though fee - bler their lays, With

vil - ioned in splen - dor, and gird - ed with praise.
sweet - ly dis - tills in the dew and the rain.
true ad - o - ra - tion shall chant to Thy praise.

The Morn of Truth Is Breaking

WEBB

Mary E. Butters

George J. Webb

1. The morn of Truth is break-ing; Ten thou - sand notes of love
2. Oh, reign in ev - ery house-hold, And where there's one soul sad,
3. Come in, thou peace-ful an - gel, And ope the gates of day;

From tune - ful souls are wak - ing To swell the songs a - bove.
Come as a ra-diant an - gel, A light to make it glad.
With beams of liv - ing love-light, Chase all things false a - way.

Come, raise a glo-rious an-them Far o - ver hill and plain,
O Truth, shine on in splen-dor! Dis - pel these shades of gloom,
Thou art that light from heav-en To glow in ev - ery soul;

For Truth in ra - diant splen-dor Has come on earth to reign.
And where there seems a des - ert, The rose shall burst in bloom.
Shine thou, O Truth! in splen-dor, As age on a - ges roll.

24 The Morn of Truth Is Breaking

MENDEBRAS
Arranged by Lowell Mason
Mary E. Butters

1. The morn of Truth is break-ing; Ten thou-sand notes of love From tune-ful souls are wak-ing To swell the songs a-bove. Come, raise a glo-rious an-them Far o-ver hill and plain,

2. Oh, reign in ev-ery house-hold, And where there's one soul sad, Come as a ra-diant an-gel, A light to make it glad. O Truth, shine on in splen-dor! Dis-pel these shades of gloom,

3. Come in, thou peace-ful an-gel, And ope the gates of day; With beams of liv-ing love-light, Chase all things false a-way. Thou art that light from heav-en To glow in ev-ery soul;

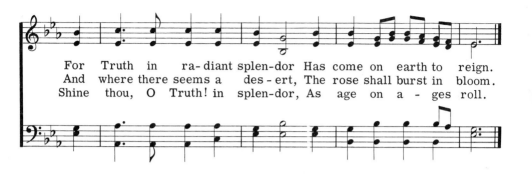

For Truth in ra-diant splen-dor Has come on earth to reign.
And where there seems a des-ert, The rose shall burst in bloom.
Shine thou, O Truth! in splen-dor, As age on a-ges roll.

Shining Words

These affirmations were chosen for display in the lobby of the Administration Building at Unity headquarters because they were the favorite affirmations of Charles Fillmore:

The joy of the Lord is your strength.

God in me is infinite wisdom. He shows me what to do.

In all thy ways acknowledge him, and he will direct thy path.

I can do all things through Christ which strengtheneth me.

Naught can disturb me, for Christ is my peace and my poise.

All things work together for good.

In quietness and in confidence shall be your strength.

Faith is the strength of the soul inside, and lost is the man without it.

The greatest teaching ever given is—Christ in you, the hope of glory.

God is my help in every need.

26 Praise to Thee, O Great Creator

John Fawcett, adapted
Stanza 2, Henry Onderdonk

BEECHER
John Zundel

1. Praise to Thee, O great Cre - a - tor!
2. Rich - es come of Thee, and hon - or,

Praise be Thine from ev - ery tongue; Oh, let ev - ery
Power and might to Thee be - long; Thine it is to

liv - ing crea - ture Join the u - ni - ver - sal song!
make us pros - per, On - ly Thine to make us strong.

Spir - it, source of all our be - ing,
Lord, to Thee, Thou God of mer - cy,

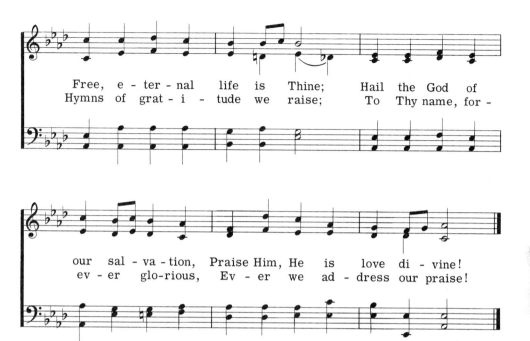

Free, e - ter - nal life is Thine; Hail the God of
Hymns of grat - i - tude we raise; To Thy name, for -

our sal - va - tion, Praise Him, He is love di - vine!
ev - er glo-rious, Ev - er we ad - dress our praise!

27   Joyful, Joyful, We Adore Thee

HYMN TO JOY
Arr. from Ludwig van Beethoven
by Edward Hodges

Henry van Dyke

1. Joy-ful, joy-ful, we a - dore Thee, God of glo - ry,
2. All Thy works with joy sur-round Thee, Earth and heav'n re -
3. Thou art giv - ing and for - giv - ing, Ev - er bless - ing,
4. Mor-tals join the might-y cho - rus, Which the morn-ing

Lord of love; Hearts un -fold like flowers be - fore Thee,
flect Thy rays, Stars and an - gels sing a - round Thee,
ev - er blest, Well-spring of the joy of liv - ing,
stars be - gan; Fa - ther love is reign - ing o'er us,

Open - ing to the sun a - bove. Melt the clouds of
Cen - ter of un - bro - ken praise; Field and for - est,
O - cean depth of hap - py rest! Thou our Fa - ther,
Broth - er love binds man to man. Ev - er sing-ing,

sin and sad-ness; Drive the dark of doubt a - way;
vale and moun-tain, Flow-ery mead -ow, flash - ing sea,
Christ our broth- er, All who live in love are Thine;
march we on - ward, Vic - tors in the midst of strife;

Giv - er   of   im - mor - tal   glad-ness,   Fill   us   with   the   light   of   day!
Chant-ing   bird   and   flow - ing   foun- tain,   Call   us   to   re - joice   in   Thee.
Teach   us   how   to   love   each   oth - er,   Lift   us   to   the   joy   di- vine.
Joy - ful   mu-sic   leads   us   sun -ward   In   the   tri-umph song   of   life.

Lord, Thy Glory Fills the Heaven   28

HYMN TO JOY
Beethoven-Hodges

Richard Mant, adapted

1. Lord, Thy glory fills the heaven;
    Earth is with its fullness stored;
    Unto Thee be glory given,
    Holy, holy, holy Lord.
    Heaven is now with anthems ringing,
    Earth takes up the angels' cry;
    Holy! holy! holy! singing,
    Lord of hosts, Thou Lord most high!

2. Praise the Lord! for He is glorious;
    Never shall his promise fail.
    God hath made His saints victorious,
    Ever Truth and love prevail.
    Praise the God of every nation;
    Hosts on high His power proclaim;
    Heaven and earth and all creation
    Laud and magnify His name.

29 Praise to the Lord, the Almighty

Joachim Neander
Translation by Catherine Winkworth
Altd. by Percy Dearmer, 1867–1936

LOBE DEN HERREN
Stralsund Gesangbuch

1. Praise to the Lord, the Al - might - y, the King of cre - a - tion; O my soul, praise Him, for He is thy health and sal - va - tion: Come, ye who hear, Broth-ers and sis - ters, draw near,
2. Praise to the Lord, who o'er all things so won-drous - ly reign - eth, Shel-ters thee un - der His wings, yea, so gen - tly sus - tain - eth: Hast thou not seen? All that is need-ful hath been
3. Praise to the Lord, who doth pros - per thy work and de - fend thee; Sure - ly His good - ness and mer - cy here dai - ly at - tend thee: Pon - der a - new All the Al - might-y can do,
4. Praise to the Lord! O let all that is in me a - dore Him! All that hath life and breath come now with prais - es be - fore Him! Let the a - men Sound from His peo-ple a - gain:

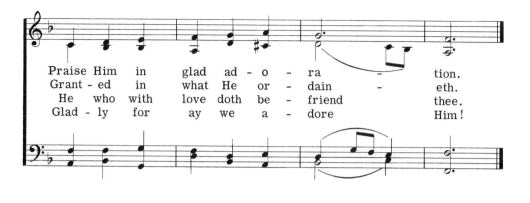

Praise Him in glad ad - o - ra - tion.
Grant - ed in what He or - dain - eth.
He who with love doth be - friend thee.
Glad - ly for ay we a - dore Him!

Alleluia

30

ALLELUIA
Jerry Sinclair

Jerry Sinclair
Refrain

Al -le - lu -ia, al -le - lu -ia, Al -le - lu -ia, al -le - lu -ia,

Al -le - lu -ia, al -le - lu -ia, Al -le - lu -ia, al -le - lu -ia.

31 Praise God

Fannie Herron Wingate

W. C. Jordan

1. If you would start the day a-right, Praise God,
2. No mat-ter what there seems to be, Praise God,

praise God. If you'd be glad from morn till night,
praise God. Though you must cross some dread Red Sea,

Praise God. If sun-shine bright-ens
Praise God. You soon will see the

all your day Or clouds loom dark a-cross your way, Yet
rain-bow's hue, For by His hand He'll lead you through, And

al-ways, as you sing or pray, Praise God!
glo-rious-ly de-liv-er you— Praise God!

Come, Thou Almighty King

ITALIAN HYMN
Felice de Giardini

32

Anonymous, adapted

1. Come, Thou al - might - y King, Help us Thy name to sing, Help us to praise: Fa - ther all glo - ri - ous, O'er all vic - to - ri - ous, Come, and reign o - ver us, An - cient of Days.

2. Come, Thou in - car - nate Word, Let all our prayers be heard, On us at - tend; Come, and Thy peo - ple bless, And give Thy word suc - cess; Spir - it of ho - li - ness, On us de - scend.

3. Come, Ho - ly Com - fort - er, Thy sa - cred wit - ness bear In this glad hour: Thou who al - might - y art, Now rule in ev - ery heart, And ne'er from us de - part, Spir - it of power.

4. To the great One in Three, E - ter - nal prais - es be Hence ev - er - more. His sov-ereign maj - es - ty May we in glo - ry see, And to e - ter - ni - ty Love and a - dore.

Keep the Heart Singing

Charles H. Gabriel

Charles H. Gabriel

1. We may light - en toil and care, Or a heav-y bur-den share, With a word, a kind-ly deed, or sun-ny smile; We may cir-cle day and night With a ha-lo of de-light, If we keep the heart sing-ing all the

2. If His love is in the soul And we yield to His con-trol, Sweet-est mu-sic will the lone-ly hours be-guile; We may drive the clouds a-way, Cheer and bless the dark-est day, If we keep the heart sing-ing all the

3. How a word of love will cheer, Kin-dle hope, and ban-ish fear, Soothe a pain, or take a-way the sting of guile; Oh, how much we all may do In the world we trav-el through, If we keep the heart sing-ing all the

Refrain

while.
while.
while.

Keep the heart sing-ing all the while;

sing-ing, sing-ing all the while;

Make the world bright-er with a smile;

bright-er, bright-er with a smile;

Keep the song ring-ing! lone-ly hours we may be-guile, If we

keep the heart sing - ing all the while.

34

Glory to God!

Mary O. Page

Clara H. Scott

1. Glo - ry to God! hal - le - lu - jahs we raise,
2. Glo - ry to God! hal - le - lu - jahs a - gain!
3. Glo - ry to God! hal - le - lu - jahs we give,

Songs of re - joic - ing we ut - ter with praise;
Pow - er from heav - en He giv - eth to men;
Hon - or the Fa - ther who taught us to live;

God in His good - ness who seek - eth to bless,
Heir with His Christ ev - ery mis - sion to bear,
One with Je - ho - vah, His love we pro - claim,

Crowns us with mer - cy and right - eous - ness.
We with His con - quests for - ev - er may share.
Let all our la - bors be sealed with His name.

Refrain

Glo - ry to God! be the end - less re - frain;
Glo - ry to God! be the end - less re - frain;
Glo - ry to God! be the end - less re - frain;

Glo - ry to God! sing it o - ver a - gain!
Glo - ry to God! sing it o - ver a - gain;
Glo - ry to God! sing it o - ver a - gain;

God in His good - ness who seek - eth to bless,
Heir with His Christ ev - ery mis - sion to bear,
One with Je - ho - vah, His love we pro - claim,

Crowns us with mer - cy and right - eous - ness.
We with His con - quests for - ev - er may share.
Let all our la - bors be sealed with His name.

35 Many and Great, O God

American Folk Hymn
Paraphrase by Philip Frazier, 1892-1964

LACQUIPARLE
American Folk Hymn

Unison

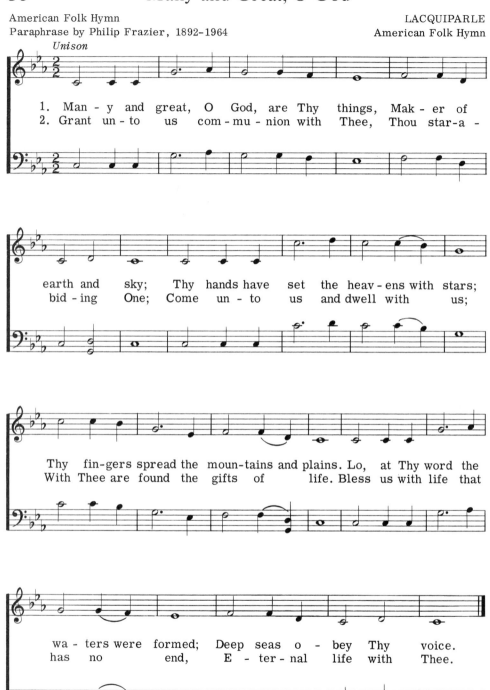

1. Man-y and great, O God, are Thy things, Mak-er of
2. Grant un-to us com-mu-nion with Thee, Thou star-a-

earth and sky; Thy hands have set the heav-ens with stars;
bid-ing One; Come un-to us and dwell with us;

Thy fin-gers spread the moun-tains and plains. Lo, at Thy word the
With Thee are found the gifts of life. Bless us with life that

wa-ters were formed; Deep seas o-bey Thy voice.
has no end, E-ter-nal life with Thee.

Praise to God, Immortal Praise

36

SPANISH HYMN

Anna L. Barbauld, adapted

Arranged by Benjamin Carr

1. Praise to God, im - mor - tal praise, For the love that crowns our days! Boun - teous Source of ev - ery joy, Let Thy praise our tongues em - ploy. For the bless-ings of the field, For the stores the gar - dens yield; For the fruits in full sup - ply, Rip-ened 'neath the sum-mer sky.

2. All that spring, with boun-teous hand, Scat - ters o'er the smil - ing land; All that lib - eral au - tumn pours From her rich, o'er - flow-ing stores; These to Thee, my God, we owe, Source whence all our bless-ings flow; And for these my soul shall raise Joy - ous songs of grate-ful praise.

37   Rejoice, Ye Pure in Heart

MARION

Adapted from Edward H. Plumptre

Arthur H. Messiter

1. Re - joice, ye pure in heart; Re - joice, give thanks and
2. Your clear ho - san - nas raise, And al - le - lu - ias
3. Then on, ye pure in heart, Re - joice, give thanks and

sing; Your voice in glad-ness raise on high, The
loud, While an - swering ech - oes up - ward float, Like
sing! Your voice in glad-ness raise on high, The

Refrain

love of Christ to bring,
wreaths of in - cense cloud.   Re - joice,   re -
love of Christ to bring!   Re - joice,

joice,   Re - joice, give thanks and sing!
re - joice,

O God, Our Help in Ages Past

Psalm 90
Isaac Watts
Stanza 3, Christina Hovemann

ST. ANNE
Attributed to William Croft

1. O God, our help in a - ges past, Our hope for years to come, Our shel - ter from the storm - y blast, And our e - ter - nal home.

2. Be - fore the hills in or - der stood, Or earth re - ceived her frame, From ev - er - last - ing Thou art God, To end - less years the same.

3. O God, Thy pres - ence here is known: Suf - fi - cient, peace - ful, sure; We trust Thy might - y power a - lone, And dwell with Thee, se - cure.

39 The Lord Is in His Holy Temple

Adaptation based on words by W. H. Bagby

J. H. Fillmore

1. The Lord is in His ho-ly tem-ple; Let earth be-fore Him si-lence keep. In rev-erence bow, ye loft-y moun - tains, And be thou still, O won - drous deep! The

2. The Lord is in your ho-ly tem-ple; De - clare the Truth in u - ni - ty; Be si - lent in His joy-ful pres - ence, Whose glo - ry fills e - ter - ni - ty. The

3. The Lord is in my ho-ly tem-ple; I speak the word in u - ni - ty; I'm si - lent in His joy-ful pres - ence, His life is my vi - tal - i - ty. The

40   Oh, Fill Me with Thy Presence, Lord

IRRADIANCE

Ernest C. Wilson

Carl Frangkiser

1. Oh, fill me with Thy pres - ence, Lord, That love may shine through me To quick - en that same pres - ence, Lord, In all whose eyes can see.

2. Oh, fill me with Thy pres - ence, Lord, That wis - dom may be mine To share Thy light with all who need To let their own light shine.

3. Oh, fill me with Thy pres - ence, Lord, To guide what power I wield, That it may ev - er strength - en good And be from ill a shield.

4. Oh, fill me with Thy pres - ence, Lord, But need I long - er wait? Thy pres - ence hath been giv - en me To live and ra - di - ate!

In the Life of Omnipresence

LIFE, LOVE, TRUTH

Geraldine D. Robinson

Pluma M. Brown

1. In the life of Om - ni - pres-ence Do I dwell,
2. In the love of Om - ni - pres-ence Do I rest,
3. In the Truth of Om - ni - pres-ence Do I stand,
4. Life and love and Truth, for - ev - er Thou art mine!

'Tis a - bove, a - round, with - in me, All is well;
Feel it fill - ing, thrill - ing through me, Bless - ed guest!
For the power of the Al - might - y Holds my hand.
Glo-rious trin - i - ty of heav - en, All - di - vine.

Life di - vine for - ev - er guid - ing All my ways,
Love di - vine all dis - cord sooth - ing In - to peace,
Truth di - vine, su - preme, un - chang - ing, All art Thou!
Oh, my soul doth sing with rap - ture Hymns of praise,

Life di - vine for - ev - er fill - ing All my days.
Love di - vine in whose sweet pres - ence Pain doth cease.
Truth di - vine, Thy word is free - dom, Spo - ken now.
And my feet shall walk with glad - ness In Thy ways.

42 This Is My Father's World

Adapted from Maltbie D. Babcock

TERRA BEATA
Franklin L. Sheppard

1. This is my Fa-ther's world, And to my lis-tening
2. This is my Fa-ther's world, The birds their car-ols
3. This is my Fa-ther's world, O let me ne'er for-

ears All na-ture sings, and round me rings The
raise; The morn-ing light, the lil-y white, De-
get That though the wrong seems oft so strong, God

mu-sic of the spheres. This is my Fa-ther's
clare their Mak-er's praise. This is my Fa-ther's
is the rul-er yet. This is my Fa-ther's

world: I rest me in the thought Of rocks and trees, of
world: He shines in all that's fair; In the rus-tling grass I
world: How could my heart be sad? The Lord is King: let the

skies and seas; His hand the won - ders wrought.
hear Him pass, He speaks to me ev - ery - where.
heav - ens ring! God reigns: let the Earth be glad!

We Come to Thee, O Lord 43

Adam Geibel

We come to Thee, O Lord, in si - lent prayer; Our

hearts to Thee, Our hearts to Thee Are o - pen

now. A - men, A - men.

44 Where Cross the Crowded Ways of Life

GERMANY

Frank Mason North

William Gardiner's *Sacred Melodies*

1. Where cross the crowd - ed ways of life,
2. In haunts of wretch - ed - ness and need,
3. The cup of wa - ter given for Thee
4. Till sons of men shall learn Thy love

Where sound the cries of race and clan, A -
On shad - owed thresh - olds dark with fears, From
Still holds the fresh - ness of Thy grace; Yet
And fol - low where Thy feet have trod; Till,

bove the noise of self - ish strife, We
paths where hide the lures of greed, We
long these mul - ti - tudes to see The
glo - rious from Thy heaven a - bove, Shall

hear Thy voice, O Son of man!
catch the vi - sion of Thy tears.
sweet com - pas - sion of Thy face.
come the cit - y of our God.

Go Not Abroad in Search of Him

MANOAH

Anonymous

H. W. Greatorex's *Collection of Church Music,* 1851

1. Go not a - broad in search of Him, To no far land re - pair, Nor to the depths of cav - erns dim, Nor heights of up - per air.

2. O gift of gifts! O grace of grace! That om - ni - pres - ent Good Makes of our hearts His dwell - ing place, In lov - ing Fa - ther - hood.

3. So wan - der not in search of Him But to thy - self re - pair, Where si - lent rev - erence reigns with - in, And thou shalt find Him there.

46   Still, Still with Thee

Harriet Beecher Stowe, adapted

Stanza 4, Anonymous

CONSOLATION

Arranged from Felix Mendelssohn

1. Still, still with Thee, when pur - ple morn-ing break - eth,
2. A - lone with Thee a - mid the mys -tic shad - ows,
3. So shall it be at last in that bright morn - ing,
4. I can - not lose Thee. Still in Thee a - bid - ing,

When the bird wak - eth and the shad - ows flee;
The sol - emn hush of na - ture new - ly born;
When the soul wak - eth and the shad - ows flee;
The end is clear, how wide so - e'er I roam;

Fair - er than morn - ing, love - li - er than day - light
A - lone with Thee, in breath-less ad - o - ra - tion,
Oh, in that hour, fair - er than day-light dawn - ing,
The law that holds the worlds my steps is guid - ing,

Dawns the sweet con - scious - ness, I am with Thee.
In the calm dew and fresh-ness of the morn.
Shall rise the glo - rious thought, I am with Thee.
And I must rest at last in Thee, my home.

Perfection

Beulah Ivon Scott

Anonymous

1. God is my per - fect life; Through Him I live.
2. God is my per - fect guide; Through Him I'm led.
3. God is my per - fect peace; Through Him I rest.

God is my per - fect gift; Through Him I give.
God is my per - fect word; Through Him I'm fed.
God is my per - fect joy; Through Him I'm blest.

God is my per - fect light; Through Him I see.
God is my per - fect good; My way is clear.
God is my per - fect will; Through me 'tis done.

God is my per - fect voice; He speaks through me.
God is my per - fect love, And He is here.
God is my per - fect all, And we are one.

48 Always with Me!

OMNIPRESENCE
Clara H. Scott

Clara H. Scott

1. Al-ways with me! I can nev-er Stray be-yond His ten-der
2. Al-ways with me! Love so ten-der Feels each trem-bling breath of
3. Al-ways with me! In His treas-ures, Free, a-bun-dant, I may
4. Al-ways with me! Ev-ery bur-den His strong arm will help me

care, For our God is om-ni-pres-ent, Here and
prayer, For our God is ev-er lis-tening, And His
share, For He holds them ev-er read-y For His
bear, For our God is om-ni-pres-ent, With His

there and ev-ery-where. Yes, ev-ery-where, and
love is ev-ery-where. Yes, ev-ery-where, and
chil-dren ev-ery-where. Yes, ev-ery-where, and
chil-dren ev-ery-where. Yes, ev-ery-where, and

slow   *a tempo*

ev-ery-where, Here and there and ev-ery-where.
ev-ery-where, And His love is ev-ery-where.
ev-ery-where, For His chil-dren ev-ery-where.
ev-ery-where, With His chil-dren ev-ery-where.

My Life Is in Thee

Clara H. Scott

Clara H. Scott

1. My life is in Thee, Thou om - ni - pres - ent One.
2. My health is in Thee, Thou om - ni - pres - ent One.
3. All power is in Thee, Thou om - ni - pres - ent One.

My life is in Thee, Thou om - ni - pres - ent One.
My health is in Thee, Thou om - ni - pres - ent One.
All power is in Thee, Thou om - ni - pres - ent One.

Foun - tain of life Thou art, Spring-ing with - in each heart;
All good I draw from Thee, Thy law pre - serv - eth me;
Thus er-ror's chains are riven; Heir of the wealth of heaven,

No life from Thee a - part, Thou Good - ness di - vine!
Help me this truth to see, And prove it di - vine.
To me, His child, is given, A free - dom di - vine.

50   I Live in the Kingdom of Light

DENNIS
Adapted by Lowell Mason
from J. G. Nägeli

W. E. Goodison-Orr

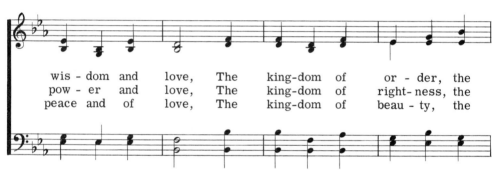

1. I live in the king-dom of light, The king-dom of
2. I live in the king-dom of life, The king-dom of
3. I live in the king-dom of God, The king-dom of

wis - dom and love, The king-dom of or - der, the
pow - er and love, The king-dom of right- ness, the
peace and of love, The king-dom of beau - ty, the

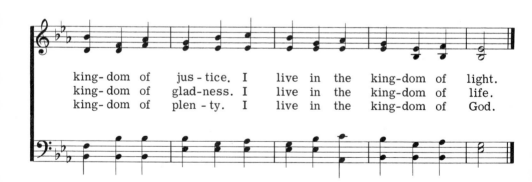

king- dom of jus - tice. I live in the king-dom of light.
king- dom of glad-ness. I live in the king-dom of life.
king- dom of plen - ty. I live in the king-dom of God.

I Lift Mine Eyes unto the Hills

51

Psalm 121, paraphased
by B. T. Jameson

WINCHESTER OLD
Est's *The Whole Book of Psalms,* 1592

1. I lift mine eyes un - to the hills, Whence com - eth all mine aid; My help now com - eth from the Lord, Who heaven and earth hath made.
2. He will not let thy foot be moved, Who doth thee safe - ly keep; For He that keep - eth Is - ra - el Doth slum - ber not, nor sleep.
3. The Lord is He that keep - eth thee, And shel - tered by His might, At noon - time or at even - tide Nor sun nor moon can smite.
4. He keeps thy soul from ev - ery ill, And safe - ly watch - eth o'er Thy com - ing and thy go - ing out Both now and ev - er - more.

52 Ever in God's Presence

Warren Meyer

ST. GERTRUDE
Arthur S. Sullivan, adapted

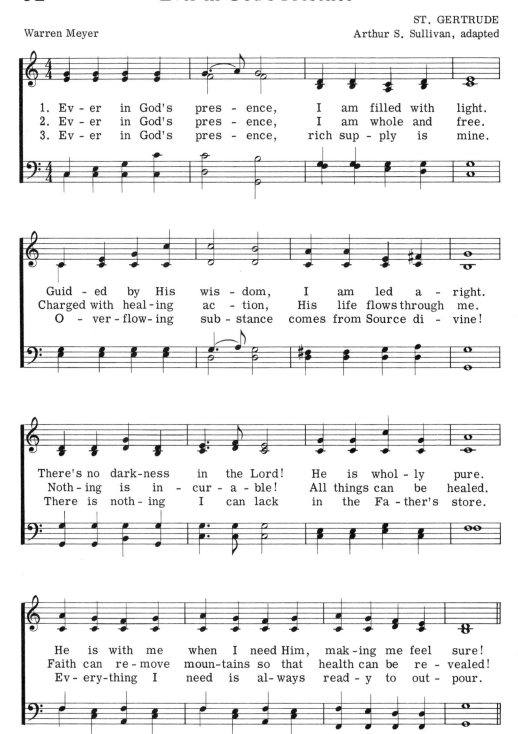

1. Ev-er in God's pres-ence, I am filled with light.
2. Ev-er in God's pres-ence, I am whole and free.
3. Ev-er in God's pres-ence, rich sup-ply is mine.

Guid-ed by His wis-dom, I am led a-right.
Charged with heal-ing ac-tion, His life flows through me.
O-ver-flow-ing sub-stance comes from Source di-vine!

There's no dark-ness in the Lord! He is whol-ly pure.
Noth-ing is in-cur-a-ble! All things can be healed.
There is noth-ing I can lack in the Fa-ther's store.

He is with me when I need Him, mak-ing me feel sure!
Faith can re-move moun-tains so that health can be re-vealed!
Ev-ery-thing I need is al-ways read-y to out-pour.

Ev - er   in   God's   in - fi -nite pres- ence   I   am   to - tal-ly

free.   I   am   al -ways   joy - ful   in   God's har - mo - ny.

The Sevenfold Affirmation   **53**

I am a child of the living God.
I have within me the all-creating power of the Christ.
It radiates from me and blesses all whom I contact.
It is my life, my strength, my courage,
My patience, my peace, my poise,
My power, my wisdom, my understanding,
My joy, my inspiration, and my abundant supply.
Unto this great power I intrust all my problems,
Knowing they will be solved in love and justice.
O Lord Christ! I have laid all my desires upon Thine
     altar, and I rest in Thy graciousness.

Adapted

54 The One and Only

Charlotte D. Maxson

CONVERSE
Charles C. Converse

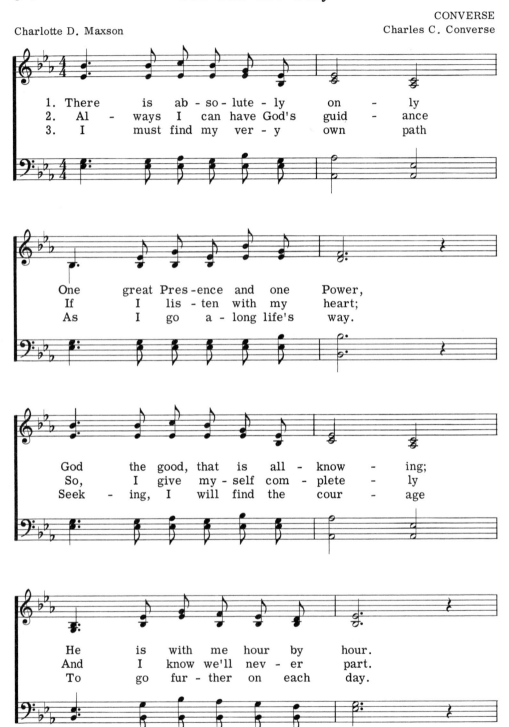

1. There is ab-so-lute-ly on-ly
2. Al-ways I can have God's guid-ance
3. I must find my ver-y own path

One great Pres-ence and one Power,
If I lis-ten with my heart;
As I go a-long life's way.

God the good, that is all-know-ing;
So, I give my-self com-plete-ly
Seek-ing, I will find the cour-age

He is with me hour by hour.
And I know we'll nev-er part.
To go fur-ther on each day.

This I know, He is all - power - ful,
Trust - ing, I am sure of an - swers
Though the world seems in a tur - moil,

He is pres - ent ev - ery - where.
To each need for which I pray.
God al - read - y has a plan.

There's no place where I'm a - ban - doned,
Trust - ing, I have all as - sur - ance
I have vi - sions of a fu - ture:

Where I go, He's al - ways there.
That my good will come my way.
All things new, in - clud - ing man!

55 Peace, Be Still

Stanzas 1 and 2, Bernice Parker Dixon
Stanza 3, Anonymous

LULLABY
Johannes Brahms

1. Peace, be still. Peace, be still. Lo, I'm with you al-ways:
2. God is life. God is love. There's none else be - side Him;
3. All is well, all is well. God is with us al-ways;

All-sus - tain - ing, ev-er - car-ing, all- a - bid-ing life and love.
All- in - dwell-ing, man-i - fest-ing all ac - cord-ing to His law.
God the Fa -ther and Moth-er is all-sus-tain-ing love.

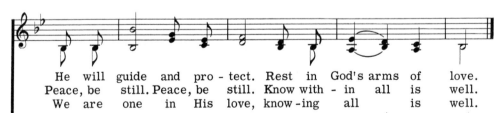

Peace, be still. Peace, be still in the pres-ence of God;
God is mind. God is power. All is at His com - mand.
We are one, we are one in the pres-ence of God.

He will guide and pro-tect. Rest in God's arms of love.
Peace, be still. Peace, be still. Know with - in all is well.
We are one in His love, know-ing all is well.

There's a Wideness in God's Mercy　56

WELLESLEY
Adapted from Frederick W. Faber　　　　　　　　　　Lizzie S. Tourjée

1. There's a wide - ness in God's mer - cy,
2. For the love of God is broad - er
3. Now our love is much more sim - ple,

Like the wide - ness of the sea;
Than the meas - ure of man's mind;
For we take Him at His word;

There's a kind - ness in His jus - tice,
And the heart of the E - ter - nal
And our lives are filled with sun - shine

Which is more than lib - er - ty.
Is most won - der - ful - ly kind.
In the pres - ence of our Lord.

57 One Presence and One Power

Unknown

Warren Meyer

There is on-ly one Pres-ence and one Pow-er

in the u - ni - verse and in me —

God, the good, God, the good,

God, the good om - ni - po - tent.

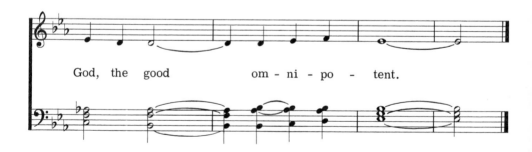

In Christ There Is No East or West 58

ST. PETER
John Oxenham
Alexander R. Reinagle

1. In Christ there is no East or West, In
2. In Him shall true hearts ev - ery - where Their
3. Join hands, then, broth - ers of the faith, What -
4. In Christ now meet both East and West, In

Him no South or North; But one great fel - low -
high com - mun - ion find; His serv - ice is the
e'er your race may be. Who serves my Fa - ther
Him meet South and North; All Christ - ly souls are

ship of love Through - out the whole wide earth.
gold - en cord Close bind - ing all man - kind.
as a son Is sure - ly kin to me.
one in Him Through - out the whole wide earth.

Words used by permission of Desmond Dunkerley, 23 Haslemere Rd., Portsmouth, England.

59 You Ask Me How Christ Comes to Me

HOW SILENTLY
Leora Carlson
Leora Carlson

Duet

1. You ask me how Christ comes to me, My
2. A tryst - ing place with Him a - lone: There
3. A - part with Him, a - lone with Him, There

heart His pres - ence fills? He comes as si - lent - ly
is no place so fair; And per - fume of the
flows in - to my heart A sweet re - pose, a

as the dawn Comes o - ver the wak - ened hills.
flowers of heaven Is borne up - on the air.
gen - tle - ness That earth can - not im - part.

Refrain

How si - lent - ly, how si - lent - ly Christ

makes His pres-ence known. 'Tis on - ly when the

soul is hushed He comes un-to His own.

I Am Stronger Than My Fears 60

LEBBAEUS
St. Alban's Tune Book, 1866
harmonized by Arthur S. Sullivan

Hannah More Kohaus

1. I am strong-er than my fears, I am wis - er than my years,
2. I am bet - ter than my deeds, I am ho -lier than my creeds,
3. He whose im - age thus I bear, And whose like-ness I shall share,

I am glad - der than my tears, For I am His im - age.
I am wealth-ier than my needs, For I am His im - age.
All His glo - ry will de-clare, Through the "I"—His im - age.

61   I Am the Way, the Truth

Marilyn E. Rieger

OLIVET
Lowell Mason

1. I am the Way, the Truth, Bring - ing to all, new youth. I am the Christ! Fol - low my light each day And you will sure - ly say, "Christ is the on - ly way For me to live!"

2. O Spir - it deep in - side, Let me Thy light ne'er hide. Thou art the Christ! Live Thou Thy life in me, In all, the good to see, And help me now to be Thy per - fect child.

3. Peace, joy, and lib - er - ty Are mine through Christ in me. Christ reigns su - preme! In Him I live each day, Ne'er from His path to stray. Christ is the on - ly way For me to live!

Words used by permission.

Fairest Lord Jesus

ST. ELIZABETH
Anonymous, adapted
Arranged by Richard Storrs Willis

1. Fair - est Lord Je - sus, Rul - er of all
2. Fair are the mead - ows, Fair - er still the
3. Fair is the sun - shine, Fair - er still the

na - ture, O Thou of God and man the
wood - lands, Robed in the bloom - ing garb of
moon - light, And all the twin - kling stars a -

Son, Thee will I cher - ish, Thee will I
spring: Je - sus is fair - er, Je - sus is
bove: Je - sus shines bright - er, Je - sus shines

hon - or, Thou, my soul's glo - ry, joy, and crown.
pur - er, Who makes the joy -ful heart to sing!
pur - er, His light in our life shines as love.

63 Begotten of God

LYONS

Marilyn E. Rieger

Adapted from J. Michael Haydn

1. O I am a son, Be - got - ten of God With
2. I praise and give thanks For all that is mine. I
3. O this is the day The Fa - ther hath made. I

wis - dom and faith, With un - der - stand - ing shod. I
show forth God's love; I let my Christ-light shine! Each
sing and re - joice For good is not de - layed. I

live in His king - dom For I am His son; I
day in His king - dom Is filled with His peace. His
am in the king - dom Of heav - en right here. Each

show forth His good - ness For He and I are one.
man - i - fold bless - ings And good - ness nev - er cease!
per - son's my broth - er And all of life so dear!

I Behold the Christ in You

Frank B. Whitney

Edna L. Gieselman

1. I be - hold the Christ in you, Here the life of God I see; I can see a great peace, too, I can see you whole and free.
2. I be - hold the Christ in you, I can see this as you walk; I see this in all you do, I can see this as you talk.
3. I be - hold God's love ex - pressed, I can see you filled with power; I can see you ev - er blessed, See Christ in you, hour by hour.
4. I be - hold the Christ in you, I can see that per - fect One; Led by God in all you do, I can see God's work is done.

65 I Behold the Christ in You

Frank B. Whitney

Bill Provost

I be-hold the Christ in you, Here the life of God I see; I can see a great peace, too, I can see you whole and free. I be-hold the Christ in you, I can see this as you walk; I see this in all you do, I can see this as you talk.

I Clothe Myself Safely Round

INFINITE LOVE AND WISDOM

Esther Marion

Clara H. Scott

I clothe my-self safe-ly round with in - fi-nite Love and Wis-dom, I clothe my-self safe-ly round with in - fi-nite Love and Wis-dom, With Love, with Love, with in - fi-nite Love and Wis - dom.

Heavenly Father, Grant Thy Blessing

A MORNING PRAYER

Fayette M. Drake

Anna Laura Drake

1. Heaven - ly Fa - ther, grant Thy bless - ing
2. Let us feel Thy liv - ing pres - ence,
3. May Thy life flow free - ly through us,
4. Fill our hearts with true thanks - giv - ing,

On each act of this glad day; Let, oh, let Thy
Fill our souls with Truth and grace; Make us all that
Pu - ri - fy us, heart and soul; Heal and har - mo -
Tune our lips to sing Thy praise; May Thy love, our

Ho - ly Spir - it Lead and guide us all the way.
Thou wouldst have us; May we see Thy smil - ing face.
nize and strength-en, Make us free, com - plete, and whole.
lives ex - press - ing, Bless and hal - low all our days.

68 The Lord's My Shepherd, I'll Not Want

Based on Psalm 23
Scottish Psalter

BROTHER JAMES'S AIR
James Leith Macbeth Bain

1. The Lord's my Shep-herd, I'll not want, He makes me down to lie In pas-tures green; He lead-eth me The si-lent wa-ters by; He lead-eth me, He
2. My soul He doth re - store a-gain, And me to walk doth make With - in the paths of bless - ed - ness, E'en for His own name's sake; With - in the paths of
3. Yea, though I walk through shad-owed vale, Yet will I fear no ill, For Thou art with me and Thy rod And staff me com - fort still; Thy rod and staff me
4. My ta - ble Thou hast fur - nish-ed In pres-ence of my foes. My head with oil Thou dost a - noint, And my cup o - ver - flows; My head with oil Thou
5. Good - ness and mer - cy all my days Shall sure - ly fol-low me, And in my Fa - ther's house al-ways My dwell-ing place shall be; And in my heart for -

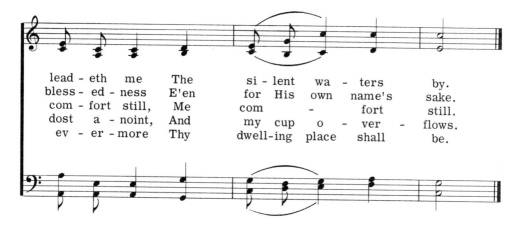

lead - eth me The si - lent wa - ters by.
bless - ed - ness E'en for His own name's sake.
com - fort still, Me com - fort still.
dost a - noint, And my cup o - ver - flows.
ev - er - more Thy dwell-ing place shall be.

Be Still, and Know That I Am God 69

Psalm 46:10

Clara H. Scott

Be still, and know that I am God, Be
still, and know that I am God, Be still, be
still, Be still, and know that I am God.

70 The Lord's Prayer

Text adapted from the Bible
by Richard D. Row, altered

FINLANDIA
Jean Sibelius
Arr. for *The Hymnal*, 1933

1. Our heaven-ly Fa - ther, who in Love a - bid -eth,
2. O give us grace to meet the com - ing mor-row;

We wor-ship Thee; we praise Thy ho - ly name.
For-give our debts as oth - ers we for - give,

Teach us Thy chil - dren ev - er-more to love Thee;
Thou leav-est not Thy chil-dren in temp - ta - tion,

Thy will be done in earth as heav'n to - day.
And from all e - vil Thou de - liv - erest us.

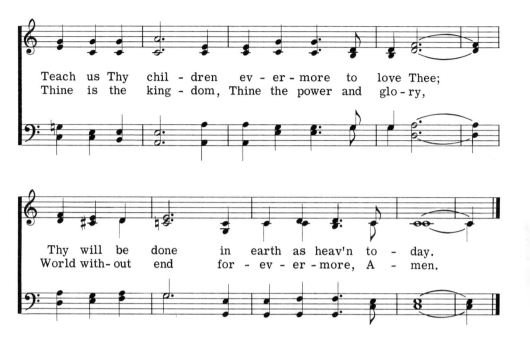

Teach us Thy chil - dren ev - er - more to love Thee;
Thine is the king - dom, Thine the power and glo - ry,

Thy will be done in earth as heav'n to - day.
World with- out end for - ev - er - more, A - men.

Take Thou My Hand 71

Adapted from Julia Sterling

From George C. Stebbins

Take Thou my hand; Lord, I am Thine.

O with Thy love now fill this heart of mine.

72   Open My Eyes, That I May See

OPEN MY EYES

Clara H. Scott

Clara H. Scott

1. O - pen my eyes, that I may see
2. O - pen my ears, that I may hear
3. O - pen my mouth, and let me bear

Glimps-es of Truth Thou hast for me; Place in my hands the
Voic - es of Truth Thou send-est clear; And while the wave -notes
Glad - ly the warm Truth ev - ery-where; O - pen my heart and

won-der-ful key   That shall un - clasp and set me free.
fall on my ear,   Ev - ery-thing false will dis - ap - pear.
let me pre-pare   Love with Thy chil - dren thus to share.

Refrain

Si-lent - ly now I wait for Thee, Read - y, my God Thy
Si-lent - ly now I wait for Thee, Read - y, my God Thy
Si-lent - ly now I wait for Thee, Read - y, my God Thy

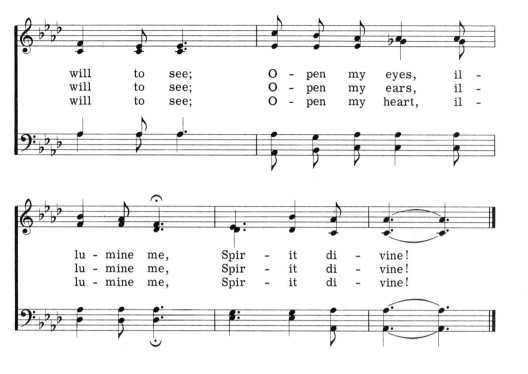

will to see; O - pen my eyes, il -
will to see; O - pen my ears, il -
will to see; O - pen my heart, il -

lu - mine me, Spir - it di - vine!
lu - mine me, Spir - it di - vine!
lu - mine me, Spir - it di - vine!

The Wonderful Love of God 73

Clara H. Scott

Clara H. Scott

The won-der-ful love of God, The won-der-ful love of God,

Be - lieve thou and trust, Trust in the won-der-ful love of God.

74 In the Silence

Bill Provost

Bill Provost

In the si-lence there is a sa-cred place,
A se-cret meet-ing place, Love is there. In the si-lence
where ev-ery co-lor blends, And ev-ery rain-bow ends,
Good is there. In the light now you find That you know

75   Dearest Father, Holy Spirit

G. Herald Keefer   G. Herald Keefer

1. Dear - est Fa - ther, Ho - ly Spir - it,
2. Strength and wis - dom, power and glo - ry,
3. God's great light and glo - ri - ous wis - dom

Bless us now as here we pray. Let Thy gra - cious,
Round us shine Thy bless - ed rays. Light of sun - shine,
Pros - pers us in U - ni - ty. Pour on us Thy

peace - ful Spir - it Bless us on this day!
peace of moon - light, Bless us on this day!
si - lent or - der, Bless us on this day!

Interlude

Dear Lord and Father of Mankind

REST

John Greenleaf Whittier

Frederick C. Maker

1. Dear Lord and Fa - ther of man - kind, For -
2. In sim - ple trust like theirs who heard, Be -
3. Drop Thy still dews of qui - et - ness, Till
3. Breathe through the puls - es of de - sire Thy

give our fe - verish ways; Re - clothe us in our
side the Syr - ian sea, The gra - cious call - ing
all our striv - ings cease; Take from our souls the
cool - ness and Thy balm; Let sense be dumb, let

right - ful mind, In pur - er lives Thy
of the Lord, Let us, like them, with -
strain and stress, And let our or - dered
flesh re - tire; Speak through the earth - quake,

serv - ice find, In deep - er rev - erence, praise.
out a word, Rise up and fol - low Thee.
lives con - fess The beau - ty of Thy peace.
wind, and fire, O still, small voice of calm.

77   Take Time to Be Holy

HOLINESS

William D. Longstaff, adapted

George C. Stebbins

1. Take time to be ho - ly, Speak oft with thy Lord;
2. Take time to be ho - ly, Be calm in thy soul,

A - bide in Him al - ways, And feed on His Word.
Each thought and each mo - tive Be - neath His con - trol;

Make friends of God's chil - dren, Help those who are weak,
Thus led by His Spir - it, Like Him thou shalt be;

For - get - ting in noth - ing His bless - ing to seek.
Thy friends in thy con - duct His like - ness shall see.

The Prayer of Faith

HURSLEY

Hannah More Kohaus

Katholisches Gesangbuch, 1774

1. God is my help in ev - ery need;
2. I now am wise, I now am true.
3. God is my health, I can't be sick;

God does my ev - ery hun - ger feed;
Pa - tient, kind, and lov - ing, too.
God is my strength, un - fail - ing, quick;

God walks be - side me, guides my way
All things I am, can do, and be,
God is my all, I know no fear,

Through ev - ery mo - ment of the day.
Through Christ, the Truth that is in me.
Since God and love and Truth are here.

79 The Prayer of Faith

Hannah More Kohaus   Bill Provost

1. God is my help in ev - ery need;
2. I now am wise, I now am true,
3. God is my health, I can't be sick;

God does my ev - ery hun - ger feed;
Pa - tient, and kind, and lov - ing, too;
God is my strength, un - fail - ing, quick;

God walks be - side me, guides my way
All things I am, can do, and be,
God is my all, I know no fear,

1, 2,

Through ev - ery mo - ment of this day.
Through Christ the Truth, that is in me.

Since God and love and Truth are here.

The Answer

When for a purpose
I had prayed and prayed and prayed
Until my words seemed worn and bare
    With arduous use,
And I had knocked and asked and
    knocked and asked again,
And all my fervor and persistence
    brought no hope,
I paused to give my weary brain a rest
And ceased my anxious human cry.
    In that still moment,
After self had tried and failed,
There came a glorious vision of God's
    power,
And, lo, my prayer was answered in
    that hour.

—*Lowell Fillmore*

81 Prayer for Protection

James Dillet Freeman

Warren Meyer

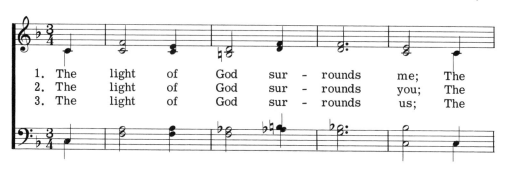

1. The light of God sur - rounds me; The
2. The light of God sur - rounds you; The
3. The light of God sur - rounds us; The

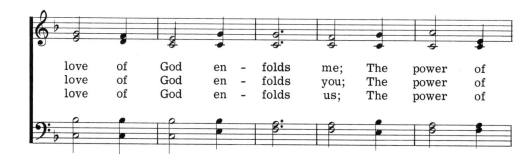

love of God en - folds me; The power of
love of God en - folds you; The power of
love of God en - folds us; The power of

God pro - tects me; The pres-ence of God watch - es
God pro - tects you; The pres-ence of God watch - es
God pro - tects us; The pres-ence of God watch - es

o - ver me. Wher - ev - er I am, God is!
o - ver you. Wher - ev - er you are, God is!
o - ver us. Wher - ev - er we are, God is!

Music used by permission.

Prayer for Protection

Adapted from James Dillet Freeman
by Carmen Moshier

Carmen Moshier

1. The light of God sur-rounds me; The love of God en-
2. The light of God shines as us; The love of God flows

folds me; The power of God pro-tects me;
as us; The power of God lives as us;

The pres-ence of God watch-es o-ver me.
The pres-ence of God now and ev-er-more.

Wher-ev-er I am, God is and all is well!
Wher-ev-er we are, God is and all is well!

83 The Light of Christ

James Dillet Freeman, adapted

Marty Haugen

The light of Christ sur-rounds us; The love of Christ en-folds us; The power of Christ pro-tects us; The

84 Prayer for Protection

James Dillet Freeman

Bill Provost

The light of God sur-rounds you; The love of God en-folds you; The power of God pro-tects you; The pres-ence of God watch-es o-ver you. Wher-

ev-er you are, God is!

Our Prayer

OUR PRAYER

Frank B. Whitney

Herbert J. Wrightson

1. I am one with God, my Fa - ther;
2. As our thought in heaven - ly plac - es,
3. We through love for - give our debt - ors,
4. I am one with God, my Fa - ther.

In the heaven - ly place we dwell. Hal - lowed is our
So on earth our will is done. From our love we
All who tres - pass we for - give. From dis - ease and
To me life and love He gives; U - ni - fied with

sanc - tu - a - ry; I'm with God and all is well.
give so free - ly Dai - ly bread to ev - ery - one.
death we res - cue, And we teach to love and live.
me, e - ter - nal In my mind and heart He lives.

86

Come Ye Apart Awhile

B. T. Jameson

POTSDAM
Adapted from J. S. Bach

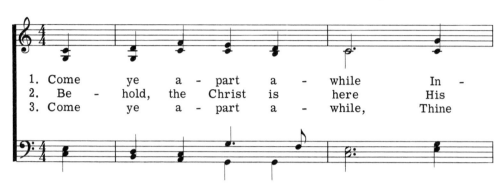

1. Come ye a - part a - while In -
2. Be - hold, the Christ is here His
3. Come ye a - part a - while, Thine

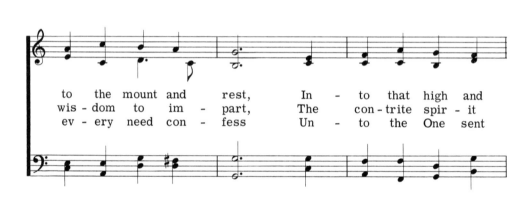

to the mount and rest, In - to that high and
wis - dom to im - part, The con - trite spir - it
ev - ery need con - fess Un - to the One sent

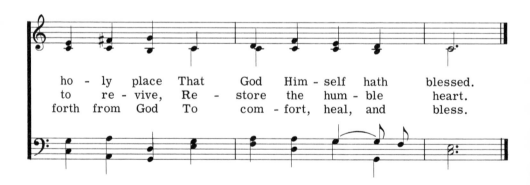

ho - ly place That God Him - self hath blessed.
to re - vive, Re - store the hum - ble heart.
forth from God To com - fort, heal, and bless.

Saviour, Teach Me, Day by Day

Jane E. Leeson

SEYMOUR
Carl Maria von Weber

1. Sav - iour, teach me, day by day,
2. With a child - like heart of love,
3. Teach me all Thy steps to trace,
4. Love in lov - ing finds em - ploy,

Love's sweet les - son to o - bey;
At Thy bid - ding may I move,
Strong to fol - low in Thy grace,
In o - be - dience all her joy;

Sweet - er les - son can - not be,
Prompt to serve and fol - low Thee,
Learn - ing how to love from Thee,
Ev - er new that joy will be,

Lov - ing Him who first loved me.
Lov - ing Him who first loved me.
Lov - ing Him who first loved me.
Lov - ing Him who first loved me.

88 Sweet Hour of Prayer

SWEET HOUR
William B. Bradbury

Anonymous

1. Sweet hour of prayer, sweet hour of prayer, In-
2. Sweet hour of prayer, sweet hour of prayer, In
3. Sweet hour of prayer, sweet hour of prayer, In-

fold - ed in the pres - ence rare Of One who fills with
love with all men ev - ery-where, The u - ni - verse is
to the "se - cret place" re - pair; I feel that quick-'ning

Truth and light, The One who works with won - drous might.
but the whole Of all that is in man's pure soul.
life of Thine And know that Thine is al - so mine.

The still - ness of this si - lent hour Brings
Through Christ, the Truth, I now be - hold The
The light of Truth is now re - vealed; I

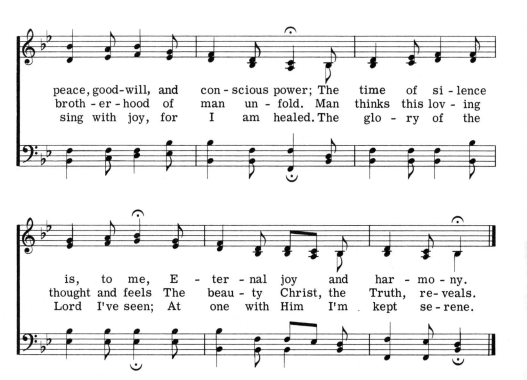

peace, good-will, and con - scious power; The time of si - lence
broth - er - hood of man un - fold. Man thinks this lov - ing
sing with joy, for I am healed. The glo - ry of the

is, to me, E - ter - nal joy and har - mo - ny.
thought and feels The beau - ty Christ, the Truth, re - veals.
Lord I've seen; At one with Him I'm kept se - rene.

89 In the Garden

GARDEN
C. Austin Miles

C. Austin Miles

1. I come to the gar-den a - lone, While the dew is still on the ros - es; And the voice I hear, Fall-ing on my ear, The Son of God dis - clos - es.
2. He speaks, and the sound of His voice Is so sweet the birds hush their sing - ing, And the mel - o - dy That he gave to me With-in my heart is ring - ing.
3. I'd stay in the gar-den with Him Though the night a - round me be fall - ing, But He bids me go; Through the voice of woe, His voice to me is call - ing.

And He walks with me, and He talks with me, And He

tells me I am His own, And the

joy we share as we tar - ry there, None

oth - er has ev - er known.

90   Build in My Soul

Warren Meyer

Traditional English Air

1. Build in my soul, O Spir-it of beau-ty, The king-dom of Christ, God's plan. O - pen my be - ing, bless all my life With the glo - ries of His true Man. O quick-en my mind with un -cloud-ed thought, My

2. Build in my soul, O in - fi - nite Spir-it, The best that pure life be - stows. Let me now speak with trans-form -ing pow - er Your Word with a faith that knows. O quick-en my mind with glo - ri - ous light, My

3. Build in my soul, O Spir-it of one - ness, Your bless-ings for me to share. Cause me to love the chil - dren of God With a free -dom be - yond com - pare. O quick-en my mind with cur-rents di -vine, My

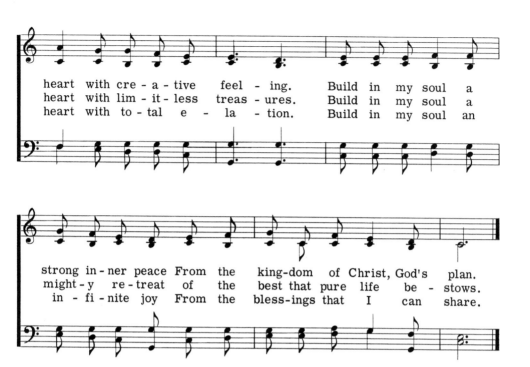

heart with cre - a - tive   feel - ing.   Build in   my soul a
heart with lim - it - less   treas - ures.   Build in   my soul a
heart with to - tal e - la - tion.   Build in   my soul an

strong in - ner peace From the   king-dom of Christ, God's   plan.
might - y re - treat of   the   best that pure life   be - stows.
in - fi - nite joy From the   bless-ings that   I   can   share.

Be Still

ST. AGNES
John B. Dykes

Herbert J. Hunt

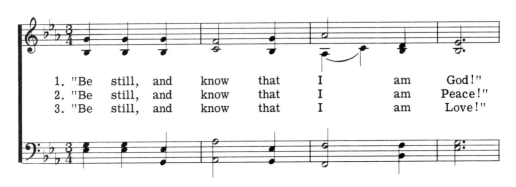

1. "Be still, and know that I am God!"
2. "Be still, and know that I am Peace!"
3. "Be still, and know that I am Love!"

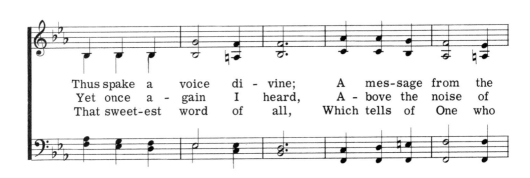

Thus spake a voice di - vine; A mes-sage from the
Yet once a - gain I heard, A - bove the noise of
That sweet-est word of all, Which tells of One who

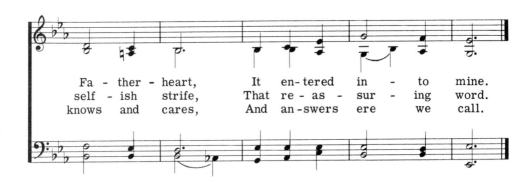

Fa - ther - heart, It en-tered in - to mine.
self - ish strife, That re - as - sur - ing word.
knows and cares, And an-swers ere we call.

Let

LET

Viva M. January

Viva M. January

1. Let God's own love now fill my heart, Let ev-ery doubt and fear de-part, Let Om-ni-pres-ence with me stay And bless and cheer and guide my way.

2. Let strength and cour-age fill my soul, Let ev-ery bur-den from me roll, Let wis-dom help me to un-fold True free-dom, peace, and joy un-told.

3. Let bod-y, soul, and spir-it be Now con-se-cra-ted all to Thee. Let all my life blend with Thy will And say to self, Peace, peace, be still.

93 The Beautiful Garden of Prayer

Eleanor Allen Schroll

J. H. Fillmore

1. There's a gar - den where Je - sus is wait - ing, There's a place that is won-drous-ly fair; For it glows with the light of His pres - ence, 'Tis the beau - ti - ful gar -den of prayer.

2. There's a gar - den where Je - sus is wait - ing, And I go with my bur - den and care; Just to learn from His lips words of com -fort, In the beau - ti - ful gar -den of prayer.

3. There's a gar - den where Je - sus is wait - ing, And He bids you to come meet Him there; Just to walk and to talk with my Sav -iour, In the beau - ti - ful gar -den of prayer.

Refrain

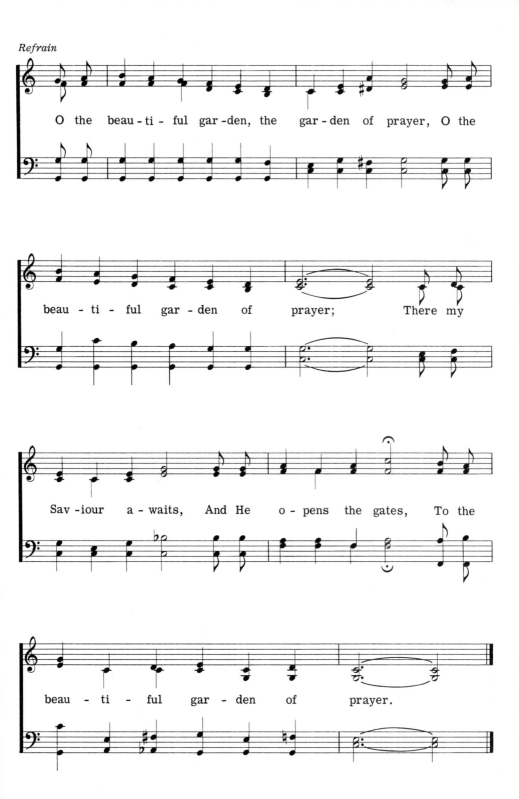

O the beau-ti-ful gar-den, the gar-den of prayer, O the

beau-ti-ful gar-den of prayer; There my

Sav-iour a-waits, And He o-pens the gates, To the

beau-ti-ful gar-den of prayer.

94   Holy Spirit, Truth Divine

Samuel Longfellow, adapted

WHITE
J. P. White

1. Ho - ly Spir - it, Truth di - vine, Dawn up-
2. Ho - ly Spir - it, Love di - vine, Glow with-
3. Ho - ly Spir - it, Power di - vine, Fill and

on this soul of mine; Word of God and in - ward
in this heart of mine; Kin - dle ev - ery high de -
nerve this will of mine; Be my law, and I shall

light, Wake my spir - it, clear my sight.
sire, Cleans - ing self in Thy pure fire.
be Firm - ly bound, yet ev - er free.

Holy Spirit, Truth Divine

MERCY

Samuel Longfellow, adapted

Louis M. Gottschalk

1. Ho - ly Spir - it, Truth di - vine,
2. Ho - ly Spir - it, Love di - vine,
3. Ho - ly Spir - it, Power di - vine,

Dawn up - on this soul of mine;
Glow with - in this heart of mine;
Fill and nerve this will of mine;

Word of God and in - ward light,
Kin - dle ev - ery high de - sire,
Be my law, and I shall be

Wake my spir - it, clear my sight.
Cleans - ing self in Thy pure fire.
Firm - ly bound, yet ev - er free.

96 Praise to Thee

Alexandra Corwin

Alexandra Corwin

1. Fa - ther-Moth-er God,   all I have is Thine,
2. Christ with - in us knows,   we are tru - ly one

1. God of all,
2. yes, we know,

for it came from Thee,
With the power of God,   whose

all is Thine,   all from Thee,
all are one,   God is power,

yet is tru-ly mine.   When I can be-lieve
lov-ing will is done.   Fa-ther-Moth-er God,

it is mine.
it is done.

and my will is Thine,
gifts and thanks we bring.

I be-lieve,   real - ly Thine,
God of all,   thanks we bring,

97 In the Stillness of the Silence

Jacqueline Neal

NORRIS
John S. Norris

1. In the still - ness of the si - lence I am one with per - fect Life. I am healed; I live in free - dom. Joy now fills me, thrills me, mind and heart.
2. In the still - ness of the si - lence I am one with Light and Love. I am wise; my thoughts are lov - ing. Peace now fills me, thrills me, mind and heart.
3. In the still - ness of the si - lence I am one with God, the good. I am trust - ing as I lis - ten. Faith now fills me, thrills me, mind and heart.

Kum Ba Yah

98

Traditional

African Folk Song

1. Kum ba ya, my Lord, Kum ba yah! Kum ba yah, my Lord, Kum ba yah! Kum ba yah, my Lord, Kum ba yah! O Lord, Kum ba yah!
2. Some-one's sing - ing, Lord, Kum ba yah! Some-one's sing - ing, Lord, Kum ba yah! Some-one's sing - ing, Lord, Kum ba yah! O Lord, Kum ba yah!
3. Some-one's pray - ing, Lord, Kum ba yah! Some-one's pray - ing, Lord, Kum ba yah! Some-one's pray - ing, Lord, Kum ba yah! O Lord, Kum ba yah!
4. I am lis - tening, Lord, Kum ba yah! I am lis - tening, Lord, Kum ba yah! I am lis - tening, Lord, Kum ba yah! O Lord, Kum ba yah!

"Kum ba yah" means "Come by here."

99 All Praise to Thee, My God

Version when sung as a canon

Thomas Ken

TALLIS' CANON
Thomas Tallis

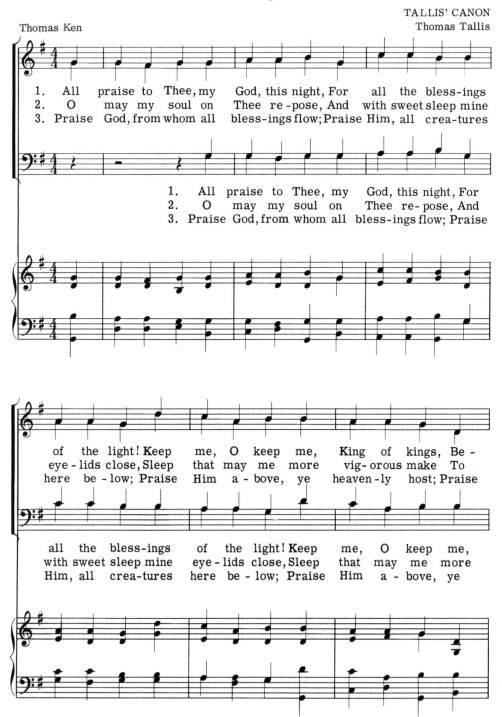

1. All praise to Thee, my God, this night, For all the bless-ings
2. O may my soul on Thee re-pose, And with sweet sleep mine
3. Praise God, from whom all bless-ings flow; Praise Him, all crea-tures

1. All praise to Thee, my God, this night, For
2. O may my soul on Thee re-pose, And
3. Praise God, from whom all bless-ings flow; Praise

of the light! Keep me, O keep me, King of kings, Be-
eye-lids close, Sleep that may me more vig-orous make To
here be-low; Praise Him a-bove, ye heaven-ly host; Praise

all the bless-ings of the light! Keep me, O keep me,
with sweet sleep mine eye-lids close, Sleep that may me more
Him, all crea-tures here be-low; Praise Him a-bove, ye

neath Thine own al - might-y wings!
serve my God when I a - wake.
Fa - ther, Son, and Ho - ly Ghost.

King of kings, Be - neath Thine own al - might-y wings!
vig - orous make To serve my God when I a - wake.
heaven - ly host; Praise Fa - ther, Son, and Ho - ly Ghost.

All Praise to Thee, My God

TALLIS' CANON
Thomas Tallis

Thomas Ken

1. All praise to Thee, my God, this night, For
2. O may my soul on Thee re - pose, And
3. Praise God, from whom all bless - ings flow; Praise

all the bless - ings of the light! Keep me, O keep me,
with sweet sleep mine eye - lids close, Sleep that may me more
Him, all crea - tures here be - low; Praise Him a - bove, ye

King of kings, Be - neath Thine own al - might-y wings!
vig - orous make To serve my God when I a - wake.
heaven - ly host; Praise Fa - ther, Son, and Ho - ly Ghost.

101 Have Thine Own Way, Lord

Adelaide A. Pollard, adapted

ADELAIDE
George C. Stebbins

1. Have Thine own way, Lord! Have Thine own way!
2. Have Thine own way, Lord! Have Thine own way!
3. Have Thine own way, Lord! Have Thine own way!

Thou art the pot - ter, I am the clay.
Search me and try me, Mas - ter, to - day!
Hold o'er my be - ing Ab - so - lute sway!

Mold me and make me Af - ter Thy will,
Pow - er, all pow - er, Sure - ly is Thine!
Fill with Thy spir - it Till all shall see

While I am wait - ing, Yield - ed and still.
Touch me and heal me, Sav - ior di - vine!
Christ on - ly, al - ways, Liv - ing in me!

Abide with Me

Adaptation by Rose E. Hulbert
from Henry F. Lyte

EVENTIDE
William H. Monk

1. A - bide with me; the dawn of day is here;
2. I need Thy pres - ence, sat - is - fy - ing, pure;
3. Hold Thou Thy Truth be - fore my won-dering sight;

Dark - ness has van - ished, light is shin - ing clear;
All else is chang - ing, Thou a - lone art sure.
Shine in my soul, fill me with life and light;

Truth's glo - rious mes - sage makes the glad earth free;
Who, like Thy - self, my guide and stay can be?
Heaven's morn - ing breaks, its glo - ry now I see;

O ho - ly Com-fort - er, a - bide with me!
Through joy e - ter - nal, Lord, a - bide with me.
Thou in rich bless-ing dost a - bide in me.

103 The God Chant

Anonymous
Anonymous

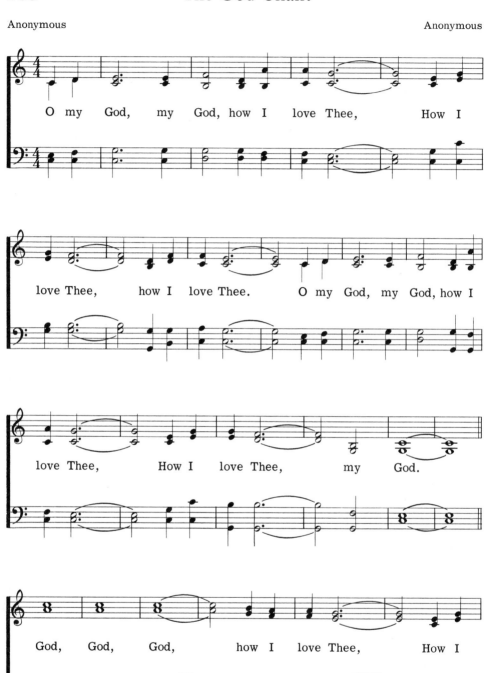

O my God, my God, how I love Thee, How I

love Thee, how I love Thee. O my God, my God, how I

love Thee, How I love Thee, my God.

God, God, God, how I love Thee, How I

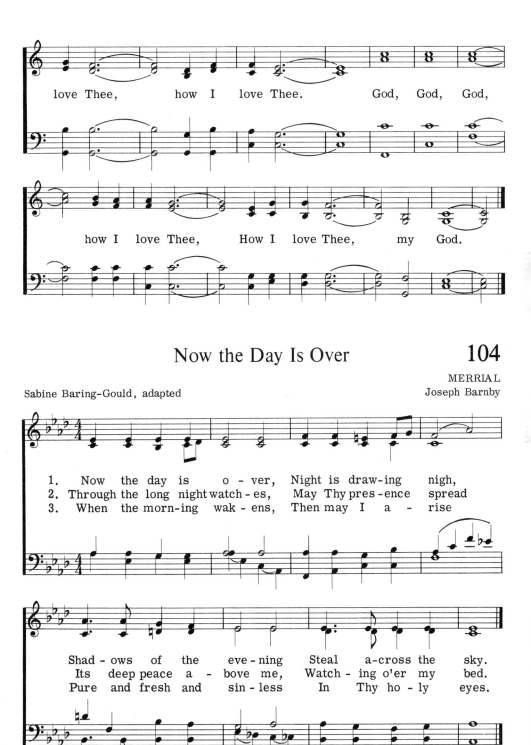

love Thee, how I love Thee. God, God, God,

how I love Thee, How I love Thee, my God.

Now the Day Is Over

104

MERRIAL
Joseph Barnby

Sabine Baring-Gould, adapted

1. Now the day is o - ver, Night is draw-ing nigh,
2. Through the long night watch - es, May Thy pres - ence spread
3. When the morn-ing wak - ens, Then may I a - rise

Shad - ows of the eve - ning Steal a-cross the sky.
Its deep peace a - bove me, Watch - ing o'er my bed.
Pure and fresh and sin - less In Thy ho - ly eyes.

105

Quietly

Warren Meyer

Warren Meyer

1. Qui - et - ly, in - ward - ly, I pause and pray;
2. Qui - et - ly, in - ward - ly, I have no fear;

God's lov - ing wis - dom now o - pens the way.
On - ly the words of the Lord do I hear.

Qui - et - ly, in - ward - ly, bath - ing in light,
Qui - et - ly, in - ward - ly, clear is my view;

I am re - ceiv - ing God's pow - er and might.
His per - fect ac - tion is mak - ing me new.

Be Still and Know

Bill Provost

Bill Provost

107 Day Is Dying in the West

Mary A. Lathbury

CHAUTAUQUA
William F. Sherwin

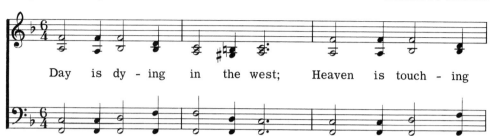

Day is dy - ing in the west; Heaven is touch - ing

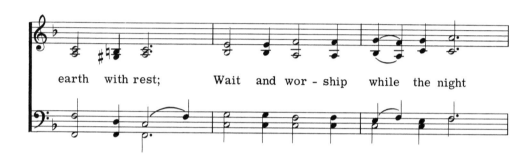

earth with rest; Wait and wor - ship while the night

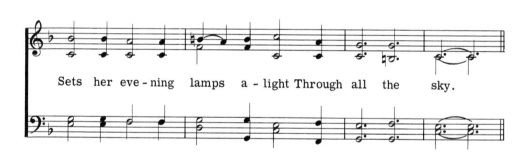

Sets her eve - ning lamps a - light Through all the sky.

Refrain

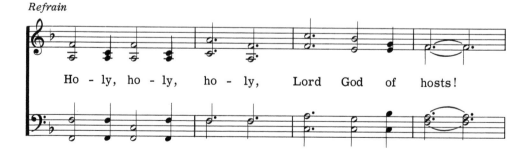

Ho - ly, ho - ly, ho - ly, Lord God of hosts!

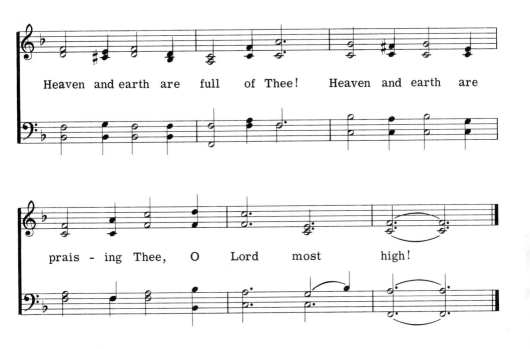

Heaven and earth are full of Thee! Heaven and earth are

prais - ing Thee, O Lord most high!

Amen

108

William Byrd

A - men.

109 Be Thou My Vision

Stanzas 1 and 2 of "A Prayer"
From *The Poem Book of the Gael:*
Selected and Edited by Eleanor Hull

SLANE
Trad. Irish Melody
Harm. by Carlton R. Young

Unison

1. Be Thou my Vi - sion, O Lord of my heart;
2. Be Thou my Wis - dom, and Thou my true Word;

Naught be all else to me, save that Thou art;
I ev - er with Thee and Thou with me, Lord;

Thou my best thought, by day or by night,
Thou my great Fa - ther, and I Thy true son,

Wak - ing or sleep - ing, Thy pres - ence my light.
Thou in me dwell - ing, and I with Thee one.

Lord, for Tomorrow and Its Needs

110

Adapted from Sybil F. Partridge
by E. R. Wilberforce

VINCENT
H. R. Palmer

1. Lord, for to-mor-row and its needs I do not pray;
2. Let me both dil-i-gent-ly work, And du-ly pray;
3. Let me be quick to do Thy will, Prompt to o-bey;

Help me, my God, to keep Thy law, Just for to-day.
Let me be kind in word and deed, Just for to-day.
Help me to con-se-crate my-self, Just for to-day.

Let me be true in all I do, In all I say;
Let me in sea-son, Lord, be grave, In sea-son, gay;
Lord, for to-mor-row and its needs I do not pray;

Set Thou a seal up-on my lips, Just for to-day.
Let me be faith-ful to Thy grace, Just for to-day.
But keep me, guide me, love me, Lord, Just for to-day.

111   Living Abundantly

WHITTLE
May Whittle Moody

Anonymous

1. Liv - ing a - bun - dant - ly, liv - ing with power,
2. Prov - ing the law as I do God's good will,

Liv - ing the Truth ev - ery day, ev - ery hour,
Prov - ing the prom - ise that faith can ful - fill,

Lis - tening to Spir - it, my way is re - vealed,
Pray - ing for wis - dom in all that I do,

Mo - ment by mo - ment, O Lord, I am healed.
Mo - ment by mo - ment, I'm one, Lord, with You.

Mo-ment by mo-ment I live in God's light.

Mo-ment by mo-ment I'm guid-ed a-right.

Ev-er re-newed in mind, bod-y, and soul,

Mo-ment by mo-ment, O Lord, I am whole.

112 God Always Helps

Evelyn Whitell

Milton Spreng

1. These words I in-ward-ly re-peat When
2. And when my path I can-not see, And
3. I speak these words mid noise and strife, When

tri-als seem too hard to meet; When thoughts of doubt rise in the
noth-ing is re-vealed to me, I know I do not need to
in the rush of cit-y life; They lift from me the weight of

way, I look them in the face and say:
fear; I stand and wait for mists to clear.
care Like prom-ised an-swer to a prayer.

Refrain

God al-ways helps, our way He guides, And His dear love each

day pro-vides; His bless-ings round a - bout us flow. O

world, lift up your head, and know God al-ways helps.

Hear Our Prayer, O Loving Father 113

MEDITATION NO. 3

G. Herald Keefer

G. Herald Keefer

1. Hear our prayer, O lov - ing Fa - ther.
2. Al - le - lu - ia, Al - le - lu - ia,

Gra - cious Spir - it, dwell in us.
Al - le - lu - ia, God is love!

114 Sonlight

Carmen Moshier

Not too fast

Carmen Moshier

1. Son - light where there seemed to be shad - ows,
2. I let my light shine and the ob - sta - cles van - ish,

Son - light where there seemed to be rain,
I let my light shine and the light casts out fear,

Son - light where there seemed to be sor - row,
I let my light shine and the ra - di - ance heals me,

Son - light where there seemed to be pain.
I let my light shine and my way is made clear.

115 Lead On, O King Eternal

Freely adapted from
Ernest W. Shurtleff

LANCASHIRE
Henry Smart

1. Lead on, O King E - ter - nal, The day of Truth is come.
2. Lead on, O King E - ter - nal, Till ev - ery war shall cease,

We fol-low in Thy foot-steps, No more in dark-ness roam.
And ev-ery-one is sing - ing the sweet a-men of peace.

Through days of prep-a - ra - tion Thy grace has made us strong,
We look be-yond ap - pear-anc-es to that which is of worth;

And now, O King E - ter - nal, We lift our joy-ful song.
We bring in love and wis - dom Thy king-dom here on earth.

In Heavenly Love Abiding

116

AURELIA

Anna L. Waring

Samuel S. Wesley

1. In heaven-ly love a - bid - ing, No change my heart shall fear;
2. Wher - ev - er He may guide me, No want shall turn me back;
3. Green pas-tures are be - fore me, Which yet I have not seen;

And safe is such con - fid - ing, For noth - ing chang- es here.
My Shep-herd is be - side me, And noth - ing can I lack.
Bright skies will soon be o'er me, Where dark- est skies have been.

The storm may roar with - out me, My heart may low be laid,
His wis - dom ev - er wak - eth, His sight is nev - er dim,
My hope I can - not meas - ure, My path to life is free;

But God is round a - bout me, And can I be dis- mayed?
He knows the way He tak - eth, And I will walk with Him.
My Sav - ior has my treas- ure, And He will walk with me.

117 Heaven Is Here

Theodosia Smith

AUSTRIA
Franz Joseph Haydn

1. Heaven is here! We find our king - dom
Formed by thought and word and deed.
May Thy grace di - vine, O Sav - ior,
Keep us faith - ful to Thy creed.

2. Heaven is here if we but claim it,
Cast a - side our wast - ed years.
Christ, our hope and strength re - new - ing,
Clears a - way all seem - ing fears.

3. Heaven is here, O praise Je - ho - vah!
If we lis - ten, we can hear
How His voice in tones com - pel - ling
Gen - tly ech - oes in our ear.

Trust - ing - ly we fol - low on - ward
Who can doubt, O bless - ed Sav - ior,
Lov - ing Fa - ther, nev - er fail - ing

To the sun - lit heights a - bove,
Walk - ing hand in hand with Thee,
When in doubt Thy chil - dren call,

By Thy ten - der care sur - round - ed,
That the glo - ry of Thy pres - ence
Sweet the man - tle of Thy pres - ence

And pro - tect - ed in Thy love.
Holds us firm in u - ni - ty!
Spreads its glo - ry o - ver all.

118   God Speaks to Me!

FINLANDIA
Jean Sibelius
Arr. for *The Hymnal*, 1933

Herbert J. Hunt

1. God speaks to me! In ac-cents sweet and ten-der,
2. God speaks to me! His voice so re - as - sur-ing,
3. God speaks to me! O let me glad-ly lis-ten

His prom-ise comes through life to be my guide;
That if I'm called to tread the shad-owed vale,
To words that cheer me all a - long life's way.

In pas-tures green and pleas-ant paths to lead me,
I'll fear no ill; His rod and staff suf - fi - cient
His heal-ing balm as - suag-es ev - ery sor-row;

With rest and shade the qui - et stream be - side.
To cope with foes, no mat - ter what as - sail.
My cup o'er - flows with mer -cies new each day!

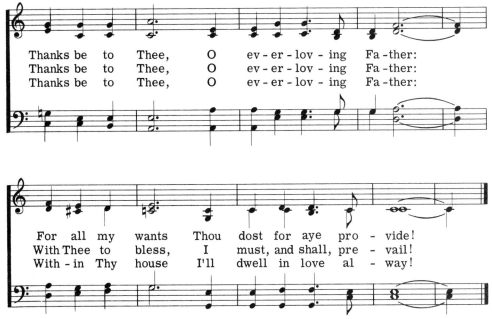

Thanks be to Thee, O ev-er-lov-ing Fa-ther:
Thanks be to Thee, O ev-er-lov-ing Fa-ther:
Thanks be to Thee, O ev-er-lov-ing Fa-ther:

For all my wants Thou dost for aye pro - vide!
With Thee to bless, I must, and shall, pre - vail!
With-in Thy house I'll dwell in love al - way!

Love Is the Only Power 119

Traditional   Traditional

Love is the on - ly pow - er, Love is the on - ly

way. Love, love, our love; How our cir-cle grows!

120   Happiness Is Found Within

Carmen Moshier   Carmen Moshier

1. Hap-pi-ness is found with-in,   hap-pi-ness I'm bound to
2. Hap-pi-ness is found with-in,   hap-pi-ness I'm bound to

win.   I can change my thoughts from gloom-y glum to glad-ness;
win.   I can change my thoughts from "No, I can't" to "can do";

Hap - pi-ness is found with - in!
Hap - pi-ness is found with -   in!   We

search and seek in out-er ways to find our hap-pi-ness, But

121   The Joy of the Lord

Based on Nehemiah 8:10
Alliene Vale

THE JOY OF THE LORD
Alliene Vale

1. The joy of the Lord is my strength;
2. If you want joy you must praise for it;
3. He giv-eth liv-ing wa-ter and I thirst no more;
4. He heals the bro-ken-heart-ed and they cry no more;

The joy of the Lord is my strength;
If you want joy you must praise for it;
He giv-eth liv-ing wa-ter and I thirst no more;
He heals the bro-ken-heart-ed and they cry no more;

The joy of the Lord is my strength;
If you want joy you must praise for it;
He giv-eth liv-ing wa-ter and I thirst no more;
He heals the bro-ken-heart-ed and they cry no more;

The joy of the Lord is my strength.
The joy of the Lord is my strength.
The joy of the Lord is my strength.
The joy of the Lord is my strength.

Love Is the Answer

Warren Meyer   Warren Meyer

1. Love! Love! Love is the an - swer;
2. Joy! Joy! Joy is the an - swer;

Love is the an - swer; Love is the way.
Joy is the an - swer; Joy is the way.

Love! Love! Love is the an - swer;
Joy! Joy! Joy is the an - swer;

Love is the an - swer; Love is the way.
Joy is the an - swer; Joy is the way.

123 Holy Light, Ignite Each Heart

SEYMOUR
Carl Maria von Weber

Elizabeth Petersen

1. Ho - ly Light, ig - nite each heart With the
2. I AM Light in whom all live; I AM
3. I AM Light! I AM the flame! With - in

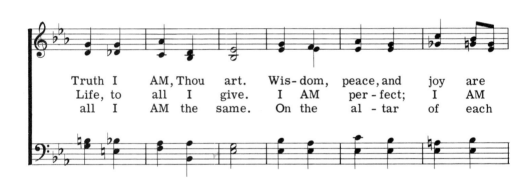

Truth I AM, Thou art. Wis-dom, peace, and joy are
Life, to all I give. I AM per - fect; I AM
all I AM the same. On the al - tar of each

mine As I AM pure love di - vine.
whole; One in bod - y, mind, and soul.
heart, Fire of love, I AM, Thou art.

I Am Listening

SICILIAN MARINERS
Sicilian Melody

A. G. Denning

1. I am lis - tening, I am lis - tening For the still, small
2. Day by day I'm learn-ing some-thing Of the pur - er,
3. When the light of Truth is shin - ing Through my mind and

voice so dear; I am lis - tening, I am lis - tening,
bet - ter way; Day by day I grow in knowl-edge
soul so clear; When my in - tu - i - tion guides me,

That my heart and soul may hear All the Truth God
Of the life, the Truth, the way, How to love and
And I know that God is here, Then no more can

is re - veal-ing To His chil - dren far and near.
help God's chil-dren Re - al - ize that bright-er day.
sor - row touch me, Then is ban - ished all my fear.

125 Work Wonders from Within

Carmen Moshier   Carmen Moshier

With feeling

Work won-ders from with - in; That's where to look, with-

in. There's no use look-ing some-where else for power that you need to

win. Work won-ders from with - in; Be sure you look with-

in. Just take your mind from out - er fears; Don't

126 A Vision

Anna L. Derschell

A VISION
Carl Moerz

1. In mo-ments rare there comes to me A vi-sion un - ex-
2. No mat - ter what life's fu - ture hours May hold of earth-born

pect - ed; I clear - ly see with - in my soul The
sad - ness, I know there comes to me in Truth A

u - ni-verse re - flect - ed. I am a part of
her - it-age of glad - ness That far tran-scends all

all that's good, I feel, I know no lim - it; The
gross - er things, I've caught the vi - sion glo - rious: We

God - in - all stands forth so clear, No fan - cied ills can dim it.
are a part of all that's good, And good shall be vic - to - rious.

God Gives Us Love 127

MEDITATION NO. 2

G. Herald Keefer

G. Herald Keefer

God gives us love, gives us love and joy and

peace; Gives us love, gives us love, gives us

love and joy and peace. *(organ)* peace.

128 All Is Yours

STOCKWELL

Mary O. Page

Darius E. Jones

1. All is yours just for the ask - ing! Ere you
2. All is yours when faith up - holds you, Sets your
3. All is yours, oh, bless - ed knowl - edge! Like the

send your si - lent plea Heaven un - locks her rich-est
won - drous spir - it free; For the might - y One has
sands be - side the sea, Or the drops with - in its

treas - ure For your wait - ing eyes to see.
prom - ised He your all in all will be.
wa - ters, Shall your man - y con - quests be.

Infinite Wisdom Guides My Way

SAXBY

Herbert J. Hunt

Timothy R. Matthews

1. In - fi - nite Wis - dom guides my way;
2. 'Tis Love di - vine that pros - pers me,
3. In con - scious un - ion, Lord, with Thee,

My path ap - pears as bright as day!
Health and all good a - bun - dant - ly;
Thy bless - ing now is given to me;

God leads me on, and gives me strength,
With sub - stance rich my life is blest,
The heaven - ly win - dows o - pen wide,

As - sured I shall ar - rive at length.
And in God's care I find sweet rest.
My ut - most needs are all sup - plied!

Words used by permission of Fern Irene Hunt.

130   I'm Healed, Praise God, I'm Healed

DENNIS
J. G. Nägeli
Arranged by Lowell Mason

Anonymous

1. I'm healed, praise God, I'm healed, Through Je - sus
2. I see, praise God, I see, Through Je - sus
3. I'm rich, praise God, I'm rich, Through Je - sus
4. I'm whole, praise God, I'm whole, Through Je - sus
5. I'm free, praise God, I'm free, Through Je - sus

Christ I'm healed; Through God, the ev - er -
Christ I see; Through God, the ev - er -
Christ I'm rich; Through God, the ev - er -
Christ I'm whole; Through God, the ev - er -
Christ I'm free; Through God, the ev - er -

last - ing good, I'm healed, praise God, I'm healed.
last - ing good, I see, praise God, I see.
last - ing good, I'm rich, praise God, I'm rich.
last - ing good, I'm whole, praise God, I'm whole.
last - ing good, I'm free, praise God, I'm free.

We Have Heard the Joyful Sound 131

Adaptation based on a text by
Priscilla J. Owens

JESUS SAVES
William J. Kirkpatrick

1. We have heard the joy-ful sound; Je-sus heals! Je-sus heals!
2. Waft it on the roll-ing tide; Je-sus heals! Je-sus heals!
3. Give the winds a might-y voice; Je-sus heals! Je-sus heals!

Spread the ti-dings all a-round; Je-sus heals! Je-sus heals!
Tell to na-tions far and wide; Je-sus heals! Je-sus heals!
Let the na-tions now re-joice; Je-sus heals! Je-sus heals!

Bear the news to ev-ery land Till the earth in hom-age kneels;
Sing ye is-lands of the sea, Till man-kind the glo-ry feels,
Shout the ti-dings full and free, Christ His love to man re-veals;

On-ward! 'tis the Lord's com-mand; Je-sus heals! Je-sus heals!
Earth shall keep her ju-bi-lee; Je-sus heals! Je-sus heals!
This our song of vic-to-ry — Je-sus heals! Je-sus heals!

132   I Am Healed

Bill Provost   Bill Provost

Unison Refrain
Slowly

God and I are one.

God and I are one. *Fine*

Verses

1. God is love; then I must be lov-ing.
2. God is life; then I must be liv-ing.
3. God is faith; then I must be faith-ful.
4. God is peace; then I must be peace-ful.

I let the love of God flow through me now, and
I let the life of God flow through me now, and
I let the faith of God flow through me now, and
I let the peace of God flow through me now, and

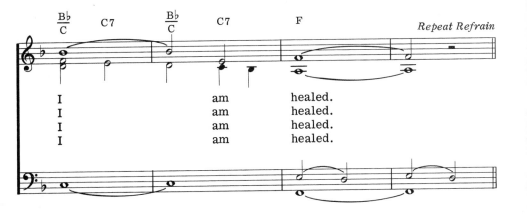

I am healed.
I am healed.
I am healed.
I am healed.

The Power to Heal

133

Shanti Ken
Arr. by ReBecca Oswald

J. Sig Paulson

The pow - er to heal, to pros - per, to guide you Is

not in the sky, it's deep down in - side you!

134 Know the River of Health Is Truth

Neil McGinness

RIVER OF HEALING
Carl Frangkiser

1. Know the riv-er of health is Truth, Deep with-in us glow - ing. From the real pres-ence, the liv - ing God, This great life stream is flow - ing.
2. Cleanse your-self in this heal - ing stream, With its power for - giv - ing, All of the thoughts and the acts that keep From us our per - fect liv - ing.
3. Do not wait for an - oth - er day. With a will un - bend - ing, Make this the hour of ac - cept - ing Him And His pure life un - end - ing.

Refrain

Flow, flow, riv - er of heal - ing, Bless - ing great - er than wealth.

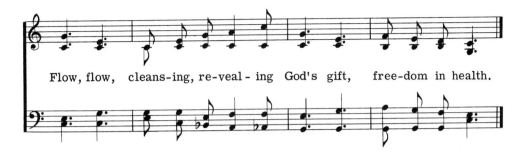

Flow, flow, cleans-ing, re-veal-ing God's gift, free-dom in health.

Healed by the Power Divine 135

Charles Fillmore

Unity Song Selections

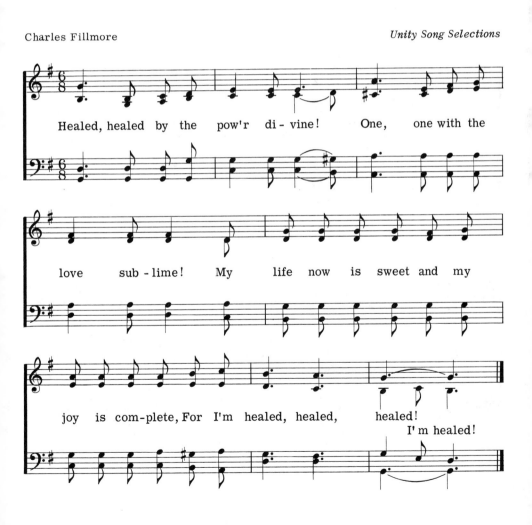

Healed, healed by the pow'r di-vine! One, one with the love sub-lime! My life now is sweet and my joy is com-plete, For I'm healed, healed, healed! I'm healed!

136 God's Holy Presence Is in Me

Francis J. Gable

HIS LIFE IN ME
Carl Frangkiser

1. God's ho-ly pres-ence is in me,
2. God made my bod-y His tem-ple,
3. My heart is filled with thanks-giv-ing,

His life in me makes me whole. His love out-pours,
Sa-cred and ho-ly and pure; With Spir-it filled,
Glad-ly to Him I give praise; His ten-der care

free-ly re-stores Bod-y and mind and soul.
glad-ly I build Health that shall long en-dure.
an-swers my prayer, Guides me in all my ways.

His life is in me, From bond - age I'm free, New foun - tains of health are re - vealed. His breath fills me through, He gives life a - new, In Him I am blessed and healed.

137 He Healeth Me! O Blessed Thought

Freely adapted from
Joseph H. Gilmore

HE LEADETH ME
William B. Bradbury

1. He heal - eth me! O bless - ed thought, O
2. Lord, I would feel Thy life in mine, To

words with heaven - ly com - fort fraught; What -
thrill my soul with love di - vine, To

e'er I do, wher - e'er I be, Still
bind me clos - er still to Thee, Since

'tis God's love that heal - eth me.
'tis Thy love that heal - eth me.

Refrain

He heal - eth me! He heal - eth me! By
His own power He heal - eth me; His
om - ni - pres - ent good I see, For
by His power He heal - eth me.

138 Hear the Footsteps of Jesus

Adaptation of text by
William J. Kirkpatrick

BE MADE WHOLE
William J. Kirkpatrick

1. Hear the foot-steps of Je - sus, He is now pass-ing by,
2. 'Tis the voice of the Sav-iour, Whose mer - ci - ful call
3. Bless - ed Sav-iour, as - sist us To rest on Thy word;

Bear - ing balm and com - pas - sion, Heal-ing all who ap - ply;
Free - ly of - fers sal - va - tion To one and to all.
May the soul-heal-ing pow - er On us now be out - poured.

As He spake to the loved one He found at the pool,
Lo! the Sav - iour stands wait - ing To strength-en your soul;
Wash us now, cleanse and quick - en, Take per - fect con - trol;

He is say - ing this mo - ment: "O be thou made whole."
He is ear - nest - ly say - ing: "O be thou made whole."
Say to each trust-ing spir - it: "Thy faith makes thee whole."

O be thou made whole, O be thou made whole; Come
O be thou made whole, O be thou made whole; Come
O I am made whole! O I am made whole! I am

in - to His pres - ence, O come ev - ery soul. See, the
in - to His pres - ence, O come ev - ery soul. See, the
quick-ened and strength-ened, Mind, bod - y, and soul. Through me

life-stream is flow - ing, See, the cleans-ing waves roll, Step
life-stream is flow - ing, See, the cleans-ing waves roll, Step
now flows the life-stream, Free, its cleans-ing waves roll, I

in - to the cur - rent And thou art made whole.
in - to the cur - rent And thou art made whole.
en - ter the cur - rent And I am made whole!

139   There Is Life, Life, Health-creating Life

Anonymous   Anonymous

1. There is life, life, health-cre-at-ing life; There is
2. There is pow'r, pow'r, won-der-work-ing pow'r; There is
3. There is peace, peace, har-mo-niz-ing peace; There is
4. There is joy, joy, soul-in-spir-ing joy; There is
5. There is strength, strength, all-sus-tain-ing strength; There is
6. There is love, love, nev-er-fail-ing love; There is

life, there is life, Life, life,
pow'r, there is pow'r, Pow'r, pow'r,
peace, there is peace, Peace, peace,
joy, there is joy, Joy, joy,
strength, there is strength, Strength, strength,
love, there is love, Love, love,

health-cre-at-ing life In the spo-ken Word of God.
won-der-work-ing pow'r In the spo-ken Word of God.
har-mo-niz-ing peace In the spo-ken Word of God.
soul-in-spir-ing joy In the spo-ken Word of God.
all-sus-tain-ing strength In the spo-ken Word of God.
nev-er-fail-ing love In the spo-ken Word of God.

Our Father Never Faileth

140

WEBB

Hannah More Kohaus

George J. Webb

1. Our Fa - ther nev - er fail - eth To give His chil - dren bread;
2. Our Fa - ther nev - er fail - eth To give His off - spring strength;
3. Our Fa - ther, God, the On - ly, Is 'round and in us all,

They on - ly need to hun - ger, More rich - ly to be fed;
They need but lean, to meas - ure Its height and breadth and length.
Sus - tain - ing and em - brac - ing, That none need ev - er fall.

For Love's a - bun - dant ta - ble Most gra - cious - ly sup - plies
"Lo, I am with you al - ways!" This is the prom - ise true,
He's light and joy and heal - ing, Oh, come and taste and see;

Each ear - nest as - pi - ra - tion, That hour - ly doth a - rise.
That knows no shade nor turn - ing, Be - lov - ed, meant for you.
Our Fa - ther fail - eth nev - er Through - out e - ter - ni - ty.

141 I See Abundance Everywhere

Theodosia Smith

BEULAH LAND
John R. Sweney

1. I see a-bun-dance ev-ery-where, God's rich sup-ply be-yond com-pare; 'Tis ours to use and to en-joy, His gift to us, with-out al-loy.

2. I pray that I may ev-er be In sweet com-mun-ion, Lord, with Thee. Up-held, pro-tect-ed by Thy hand, Se-cure in Thy dear care I stand.

3. There is no lack! All-boun-ti-ful, His love pro-vides. How beau-ti-ful To know God guides us on our way, Sus-tains and bless-es us each day!

Refrain

Pros - per - i - ty, pros - per - i - ty, I know my own shall come to me. God sends His chil - dren joy and peace, Good health and wis - dom and in - crease, And we our grate - ful voic - es raise To Thee, O God, in hymns of praise.

142   Thou Art the Source of All Good

ITALIAN HYMN

Marilyn E. Rieger   Felice de Giardini

1. Thou art the source of all good: Wis - dom, true
2. Liv - ing for Christ ev - ery day, Let - ting His
3. Break forth, O ra - diant Light! Scat - ter the

love and broth - er - hood. Thou art the Christ!
Spir - it guide my way In - to all Truth!
shad - ows of night. Shine, bright - ly shine

Dwell-ing with - in my heart, Nev - er from me to part.
I am now whole and free, With strength, vi - tal - i - ty,
In - to each dark - ened place. Bring to each wea - ry face

Help me this day to start Liv - ing for Thee!
And per - fect har - mo - ny — All things made new!
Vic - to - ry, joy, and grace. Shine, bright - ly shine!

Prosperity Is Mine

Warren Meyer

Warren Meyer

Pros - per - i - ty is mine; Pros-

per - i - ty is mine; Pros -

per - i - ty, Pros - per - i - ty, Pros -

per - i - ty is mine.

144   Now Are the Showers of Blessings

Unity Song Selections
Adapted from D. W. Whittle

SHOWERS OF BLESSING
James McGranahan

1. Now are the show-ers of bless - ings
2. Now are the show-ers of bless - ings,
3. Boun - ti - ful meas - ure ful - fill - ing,

Sent by the Fa-ther of love; Now is the time of ex -
Meet-ing our mo-ment-ly need; Now are the rich-es of
Pour-ing up-on us, O Lord! Now are the show-ers of

press - ing   Boun - ti - ful gifts from a - bove.
heav - en,   Heal -ing our hearts of all greed.
bless - ings,   Prom - is - es made by Thy Word.

Refrain

Show - ers of bless-ings, Show-ers of bless-ings in store;

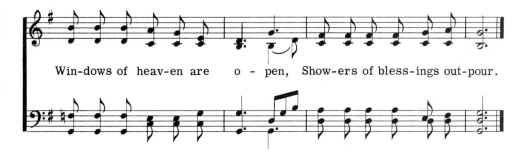

Win-dows of heav-en are o - pen, Show-ers of bless-ings out-pour.

Sweep Over My Soul

145

Harry D. Clarke

Harry D. Clarke

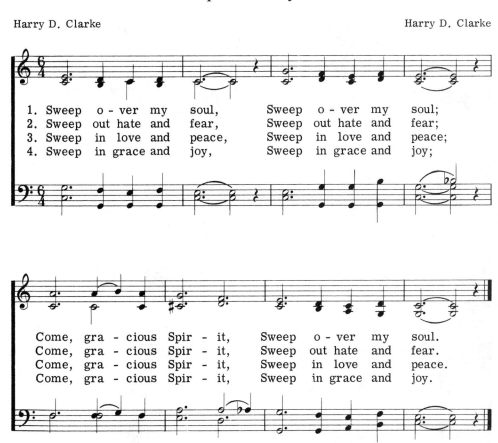

1. Sweep o - ver my soul, Sweep o - ver my soul;
2. Sweep out hate and fear, Sweep out hate and fear;
3. Sweep in love and peace, Sweep in love and peace;
4. Sweep in grace and joy, Sweep in grace and joy;

Come, gra - cious Spir - it, Sweep o - ver my soul.
Come, gra - cious Spir - it, Sweep out hate and fear.
Come, gra - cious Spir - it, Sweep in love and peace.
Come, gra - cious Spir - it, Sweep in grace and joy.

146 Prosperity

Francis J. Gable

PROSPERITY
Carl Frangkiser

1. From the Fa-ther's store Rich-es now out-pour For the
2. Heav-en's door is wide; And the end-less tide Of the
3. By His law we live, And we free-ly give Of the

one who will be - lieve, Who can un-der-stand From His
Fa-ther's love and wealth Flows, a might-y stream, On whose
good that God be - stows. Thus a rich sup-ply Of His

o - pen hand Come the bless-ings we re - ceive.
wa - ters gleam True pros-per-i-ty and health.
wealth is nigh, For our need the Fa-ther knows.

Refrain

I am pros-pered Tru-ly pros-pered, By His

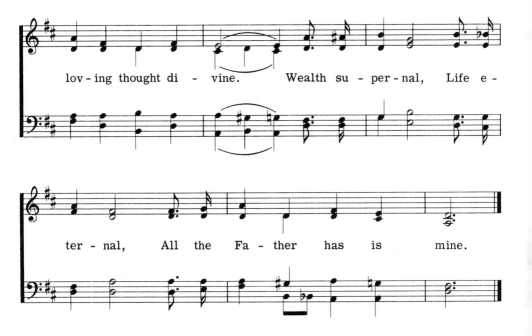

lov - ing thought di - vine. Wealth su - per - nal, Life e - ter - nal, All the Fa - ther has is mine.

The Hope of Glory   **147**

Christ is the light of my mind;
Illumined are my thoughts.
Christ is the love of my heart;
Compassionate are my words.
Christ is the strength of my hands;
Helpful are my deeds.
Christ is the power of my legs;
Effortlessly I walk His path.
Christ is the understanding of my eyes;
Pure is my vision.
Christ in me my all;
Christ in all I see.

—Ric Schumacher

148

I'm Rich in Thee

Russell Kemp

HE LEADETH ME
William B. Bradbury

1. There is no lack, no pov - er - ty: Thy
2. Lord, I would feel Thy sub - stance fine, En -
3. I have re - ceived, I thank Thee, Lord, My

well of plen - ty flows for me. What -
rich my soul with wealth di - vine, So
soul with heaven - ly wealth is stored, All

e'er I do, what - e'er I see, There
bless my words that I may see There
praise to Thee, all praise to Thee; There

is no lack, I'm rich in Thee.
is no lack, I'm rich in Thee.
is no lack, I'm rich in Thee.

Refrain

I'm rich in Thee, I'm rich in Thee, Thy well of plen - ty flows for me. Thy wealth of sub - stance now I see; There is no lack, I'm rich in Thee.

149

My Source

BRING THEM IN

Christina Hovemann

William Ogden

1. God is the source of my sup-ply,
2. God has a-bun-dant-ly de-creed
3. "Prove me and see, now, if I will

Read-y the good to mul-ti-ply, Bring-ing the sub-stance
Sub-stance sup-ply-ing ev-ery need, Caus-ing His rich-es
Win-dows of heav-en o-pen, 'til So man-y won-drous

I re-quire, Fill-ing my ev-ery deep de-sire.
to out-pour 'Til ev-ery cup is run-ning o'er.
bless-ings pour, There won't be room e-nough for more!"

Refrain

This, I know: bless-ings flow, And my con-fi-dence in

God will grow; Yes, I know: bless-ings flow,

Fill - ing ev - ery deep de - sire.

O May My Life

150

From John Monsell

Adapted from WARWICK
Samuel Stanley

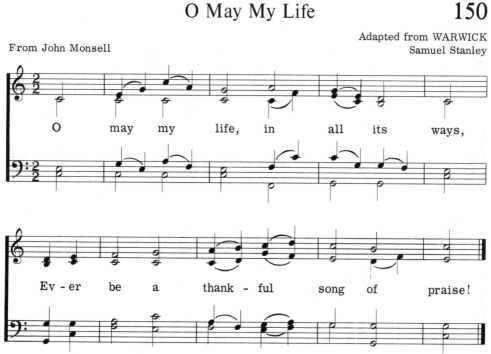

O may my life, in all its ways,

Ev - er be a thank - ful song of praise!

151 There Shall Be Showers of Blessing

SHOWERS OF BLESSING

Daniel W. Whittle

James McGranahan

1. "There shall be show-ers of bless - ing:"
2. "There shall be show-ers of bless - ing,"
3. "There shall be show-ers of bless - ing,"

This is the prom-ise of love; There shall be sea-sons re-
Pre-cious re - viv - ing a - gain; O - ver the hills and the
Send them up - on us, O Lord; Grant to us now a re-

fresh - ing, Sent from the Sav - iour a - bove.
val - leys, Sound of a - bun-dance of rain.
fresh - ing, Come, and now hon - or Thy Word.

Refrain

Show - ers of bless - ing, Show-ers of bless-ing we need;

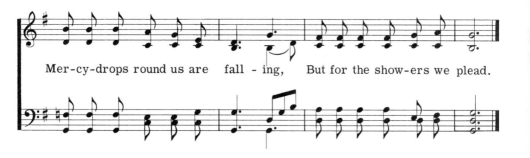

Mer-cy-drops round us are fall-ing, But for the show-ers we plead.

Only Believe 152

Paul Rader
ONLY BELIEVE
Paul Rader

On - ly be - lieve, on - ly be - lieve; All things are pos-si-ble, on-ly be - lieve; On - ly be - lieve, on - ly be - lieve; All things are pos-si- ble, on - ly be - lieve.

153   Count Your Blessings

Adapted version based on
Johnson Oatman, Jr.

BLESSINGS
Edwin O. Excell

1. When up-on life's bil-lows you seem tem-pest - tossed,
2. When your life seems emp-ty, it is so un - true;

When you feel dis - cour-aged, think-ing all is lost,
There's a might-y Pres-ence mak-ing all things new.

Count your man - y bless-ings, name them one by one,
Mir - a - cles take place wher-ev - er you may be,

And it will sur - prise you what the Lord has done.
Prov-ing that God's love is with you con - stant - ly.

Refrain

Count your bless-ings, Name them one by one;

Count your bless-ings, See what God has done;

Count your bless-ings, Name them one by one;

Count your man-y bless-ings, See what God has done.

154 Prosperity Now

Bill Provost   Bill Provost

Counter-melody, optional

O -pen up your heart   and

Refrain   F   Bb7   D7   G7   C7

Pros-per -i - ty,   pros - per -i - ty,

sing;   Let   the mu - sic   flow

F   G7   C7   F   Bb7

pros - per - i - ty   now;   Pros-per -i -ty,

a -   long.   Hal - le-lu -jah!

D7   G7   C7   F   G7   Gm

pros -   per-i-ty,   Let me show you   how —

155   This Is My Father's World

Carmen Moshier   Carmen Moshier

Stanzas 1–3, moderately fast (in 2)
Stanza 4, slower (in 4)

1. This is my Fa - ther's world, flowers and birds and
2. This is my Fa - ther's world, rich be - yond com -
3. This is my Fa - ther's world, to the far - thest
4. This is my Fa - ther's world, ev - ery man di -

trees, This is my Fa - ther's world,
pare, This is my Fa - ther's world,
star, This is my Fa - ther's world,
vine, This is my Fa - ther's world,

chil - dren, you and me! This is my
no lack an - y - where, This is my
whole-ness near and far. This is my
son of God de - sign. This is my

Fa - ther's world, it's mine when I know
Fa - ther's world, it's mine when I know
Fa - ther's world, it's mine when I know
Fa - ther's world, it's mine when I know

156 Song of Faith

B. Y. Williams

Alice Morse Glover

1. I shall not fear; The ter-rors that con - found me
2. I shall not want; How could that thought as - sail me,

Van - ish at length, like mists be - fore the
Know - ing His wealth is in - fi - nite in -

sun. Know - ing His arm is ev - er-more a -
deed? How could I think His love would ev - er

round me, What need I fear, what per - ils need I shun?
fail me, Or dream His boun - ty would not meet my need?

I shall not fail, Nor shall my task ap-

pall me, Though it may seem too heav-y for my

hands; I know that He who to the task did

call me Will give me strength to meet the task's de-mands.

157   Holy Spirit, Source of Gladness

Paul Gerhardt
Translation, adapted

ELLESDIE
Arranged from W. A. Mozart

1. Ho - ly Spir - it, Source of glad - ness!
   Come with all Thy ra - diance bright; O'er our sense of
   toil and sad - ness Breathe Thy life and
   shed Thy light. Send us Thine il - lu - mi - na - tion;

2. Let the peace which knows no meas - ure,
   Now in quick-ening showers de - scend, Bring-ing us the
   rich - est treas - ure Man can wish or
   God can send. With a faith-filled af - fir - ma - tion,

Ban - ish all our soul's an - noy; Rest up - on this
Ev - ery fear we now re - lease; Rest up - on this

con - gre-ga - tion, Spir - it of un - fail - ing joy!
con - gre-ga - tion, Spir - it of un - trou - bled peace!

I Know the Lord 158

Traditional   Traditional

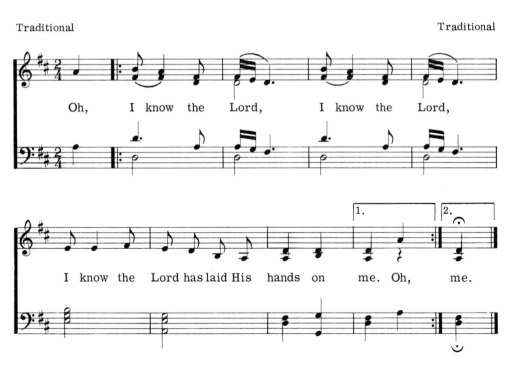

Oh, I know the Lord, I know the Lord,

I know the Lord has laid His hands on me. Oh, me.

159 Confident Living

ASSURANCE
Warren Meyer
Phoebe P. Knapp

1. Con - fi - dent liv - ing, ban - ner of might, Comes from the Spir - it with glo - ri - ous light. Con - fi - dent liv - ing cleans - es my soul, Giv - ing the Spir - it full - est con - trol.

2. Con - fi - dent liv - ing helps me ex - pand Vi - sions of val - ue, the king-dom at hand. Con - fi - dent liv - ing, tal - ent to win, Gift of the Spir - it moves from with - in.

3. Con - fi - dent liv - ing keeps me a - ware Ev - er that true love is found ev - ery-where. Con - fi - dent liv - ing ful - fills my way, O - pens my chan - nels with - out de - lay.

Refrain

Con - fi - dent liv - ing rights ev - ery wrong; Dy - nam - ic pow - er helps me be strong. Con - fi - dent liv - ing com - forts my heart; From such a bless - ing I can't de - part.

160   Faith Is the Victory

Adapted from John H. Yates   Ira D. Sankey

1. En - camped a - long the hills of light, Ye
2. His ban - ner o - ver us is love, Our
3. On ev - ery hand God's Truth we find Drawn

Chris - tian sol - diers, rise, And let your songs of
sword the word of God; We walk in paths of
up in bright ar - ray; Let thoughts of Good fill

praise and joy Be lift - ed to the skies. Know
right - eous - ness When guid - ed by His word. By
ev - ery mind, And dwell in peace to - day. Sal -

that the foe in vales be - low Is naught, for God is
faith do words of Truth and light Sweep on o'er ev - ery
va - tion's hel - met on each head, With Truth all girt a -

161 God of Our Life, Through All the Circling Years

LUX BENIGNA
John B. Dykes

Hugh T. Kerr, alt.

1. God of our life, through all the cir - cling years, We trust in Thee; In all the past, through all our hopes and fears, Thy hand we see. With each new day, when
2. God of the past, our times are in Thy hand; With us a - bide. Lead us by faith to hope's true prom - ised land; Be Thou our guide. With Thee to bless, the
3. God of the com - ing years, through paths un - known We fol - low Thee; When we are strong, Lord, leave us not a - lone; Our ref - uge be. Be Thou for us in

morn-ing lifts the veil, We own Thy
dark-ness shines as light, And faith's fair
life our dai-ly bread, Our heart's true

mer - cies, Lord, which nev - er fail.
vi - sion chang-es in - to sight.
home toward which our years have led.

162   I Dare Believe That God Is Good

ELLON

Herbert J. Hunt   George F. Root

1. I dare be-lieve That God is Good Though dark may seem the day; His kind-ly Light Makes all things bright, And guides me on my way. I dare be-lieve That God is Love, And

2. I dare be-lieve That God is Life, With joy He fills my soul! His quick-ening Word With-in is heard, And I am now made whole! I dare be-lieve That God pro-tects: Each

3. I dare be-lieve That God is All, And All He doth im-part. Him-self He gives, And ev-er lives, With-in each lov-ing heart! I dare be-lieve That God is Good Though

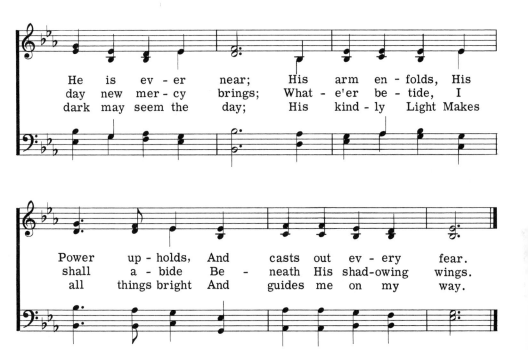

He is ev - er near; His arm en - folds, His
day new mer - cy brings; What - e'er be - tide, I
dark may seem the day; His kind - ly Light Makes

Power up - holds, And casts out ev - ery fear.
shall a - bide Be - neath His shad-owing wings.
all things bright And guides me on my way.

163 The Twelve Powers

GALILEE

Marilyn E. Rieger

William H. Jude

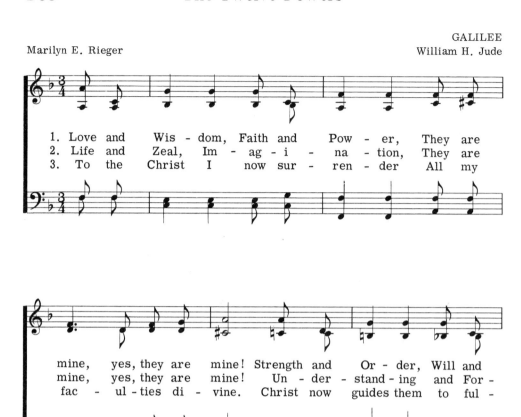

1. Love and Wis - dom, Faith and Pow - er, They are
2. Life and Zeal, Im - ag - i - na - tion, They are
3. To the Christ I now sur - ren - der All my

mine, yes, they are mine! Strength and Or - der, Will and
mine, yes, they are mine! Un - der - stand - ing and For -
fac - ul - ties di - vine. Christ now guides them to ful -

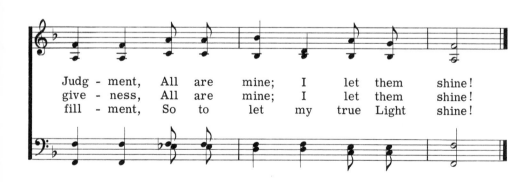

Judg - ment, All are mine; I let them shine!
give - ness, All are mine; I let them shine!
fill - ment, So to let my true Light shine!

Ask for Me

Alan Stanley

Alan Stanley

1. Ask for me, I am there!
2. Need a friend? Think of me.
3. I'm one with you, You're one with me. I'm

Ask for me, I am there!
Need a friend? Think of me.
one with you, You're one with me. I'm

Ask for me, I am there!
Need a friend? Think of me.
one with you, You're one with me.

I am there, I am there, I am there!
Think of me, think of me, think of me.
We are one, we are one, we are one.

165 God Is Love

Clara H. Scott

ALL IS WELL
Clara H. Scott

1. God is Love; that Love sur - rounds me, In that
2. God is Life; that Life sur - rounds me, In that
3. God is Health; that Health sur - rounds me, In that
4. God is Peace; that Peace sur - rounds me, In that

Love I safe - ly dwell, 'Tis a - bove, be - neath, with -
Life I safe - ly dwell, 'Tis a - bove, be - neath, with -
Health I safe - ly dwell, 'Tis a - bove, be - neath, with -
Peace I safe - ly dwell, 'Tis a - bove, be - neath, with -

in me, Love is mine, and all is well. God is
in me, Life is mine, and all is well. God is
in me, Health is mine, and all is well. God is
in me, Peace is mine, and all is well. God is

Love, pure Love, God is Love, sweet Love, That Love is
Life, pure Life, God is Life, sweet Life, That Life is
Health, pure Health, God is Health, sweet Health, That Health is
Peace, pure Peace, God is Peace, sweet Peace, That Peace is

mine, mine, and all is well.
mine, mine, and all is well.
mine, mine, and all is well.
mine, mine, and all is well.

5. God is Strength; ...   7. God is Joy; ...
6. God is Light; ...   8. God is Truth; ...

Blessings for a Child   166

Bill Provost   Bill Provost
Tenderly

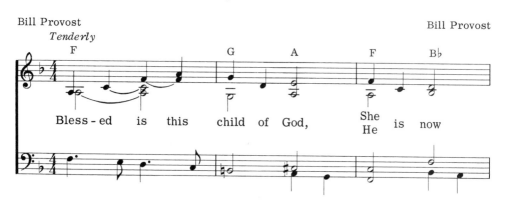

Bless-ed is this child of God,   She/He is now

filled with *love; Thank You, Fa-ther, for this child.

* Other words may be used: Light; life; peace; joy.

167 Loved with Everlasting Love

Stanzas: Anonymous
Refrain from Mary A. Lathbury

CHAUTAUQUA
William F. Sherwin

1. Loved with ev - er - last - ing love, Led by grace that
2. Oh, this full and per - fect peace! Oh, this trans - port
3. Birds with glad - der songs o'er - flow, Flowers with deep - er

love to know; Spir - it breath - ing from a - bove,
all di - vine! In a love which can - not cease,
beau - ty shine, Since I know as now I know,

Thou hast taught me it is so. How great Thy love!
I am His and He is mine. How great His love!
I am His and He is mine. How great His love!

Refrain

Ho - ly, ho - ly, ho - ly, Lord God of hosts!

Heaven and earth are full of Thee, Heaven and earth are full of Thee, O Lord, Most High!

Earth, with Her Ten Thousand Flowers 168

T. R. Taylor, adapted
Refrain from W. B. Rands

CHAUTAUQUA
William F. Sherwin

1. Earth, with her ten thousand flowers,
   Air, with all its beams and showers,
   All around, below, above,
   Speak to us that "God is Love."
   Yes, "God is Love."

Refrain:
   Holy, holy, holy, Lord God of Love.
   Love is old, and Love is new;
   Love endureth, firm and true.
   Yes, "God is Love."

169 The Bread That Giveth Strength

Adapted from Ellen H. Underwood

MORECAMBE
Frederick C. Atkinson

1. The bread that giv-eth strength I want to give,
2. I want to give the oil of joy for tears,
3. I want to give good meas-ure, run-ning o'er,
4. I want to give to oth-ers hope and faith;

The wa-ter pure that bids the thirst-y live;
The faith to con-quer crowd-ing doubts and fears;
And in-to an-gry hearts I want to pour
I want to do all that the Mas-ter saith;

I want to help the faint-ing day by day;
Beau-ty for ash-es may I give al-ways;
The an-swer soft that turn-eth wrath a-way;
I want to live a-right from day to day;

This is my place in life, to love, God's way.
This is my place in life, to love, God's way.
This is my place in life, to love, God's way.
This is my place in life, to love, God's way.

God Is Love; His Mercy Brightens

John Bowring, adapted

STOCKWELL
Darius E. Jones

1. God is love; His mer - cy bright - ens All the
2. Time and change are bus - y ev - er; Earth de -
3. E'en the hour that dark - est seem - eth Will His
4. He all earth - ly care un - bind - eth, Rest He

path in which we rove; Bliss He wakes and woe He
cays, and a - ges move; But His mer - cy wan - eth
change - less good-ness prove; From the mist His bright - ness
send - eth from a - bove; Ev - ery - where the glo - ry

light - ens; God is wis - dom, God is love.
nev - er; God is wis - dom, God is love.
stream - eth; God is wis - dom, God is love.
shin - eth; God is wis - dom, God is love.

171 O Love Divine! Where'er I Am

Hannah More Kohaus

Traditional German Melody

1. O Love di - vine! wher - e'er I am, Thou
2. O Love di - vine! what - e'er be - fall, If
3. Se - cure - ly may I trust in Thee, Thou

dost a - bide with me; What - ev - er path in
good or ill my lot; What - ev - er I may
Love di - vine so sure; Un - moved as the e -

life I take, I still re - main in Thee;
bring to pass, O Love! Thou chang - est not;
ter - nal hills, Thou dost for aye en - dure;

For Thou art here and ev - ery - where, Thou
Thou art the same un - va - ry - ing, Through-
O Love di - vine! I would be filled With

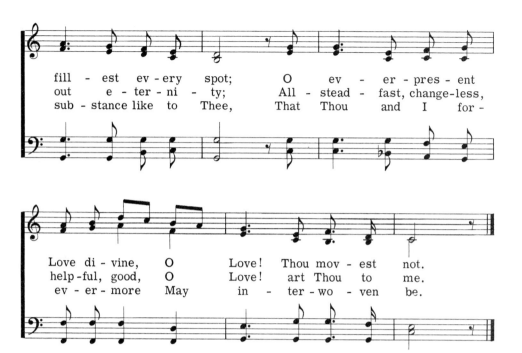

fill - est ev - ery spot; O ev - er - pres - ent
out e - ter - ni - ty; All - stead - fast, change-less,
sub - stance like to Thee, That Thou and I for -

Love di - vine, O Love! Thou mov - est not.
help -ful, good, O Love! art Thou to me.
ev - er - more May in - ter - wo - ven be.

172 Everlasting Love

EVERLASTING LOVE
Clara H. Scott

Helen L. Manning

1. Ev - er - last - ing love in - folds me,
2. Shad - ows flee be - fore faith's bright - ness,

Om - ni - pres - ent, change-less, true; Sat - is - fi - eth
Hope springs up with buoy - ant tread; Health and strength are

all my long - ings, Makes me both to will and do.
my com - pan - ions, No more weak-ness, pain, or dread.

I am here the Fa-ther's wit - ness, Might - y words of
Power comes to me in the si - lence, Fills my soul with

Truth to speak; Ban - ish er - ror, sin, and sick-ness,
rap - ture rare; Faith pro-claims o'er earth's do - min - ion,

Lift the bur - dens of the weak. Ev - er -last - ing
Wis - dom shines with jew - els fair. Ev - er -last - ing

love in- folds me, Om - ni - pres - ent, change-less, true.
love in- folds me, Om - ni - pres - ent, change-less, true.

173 Love Is a Magnet

Francis J. Gable

Carl Frangkiser

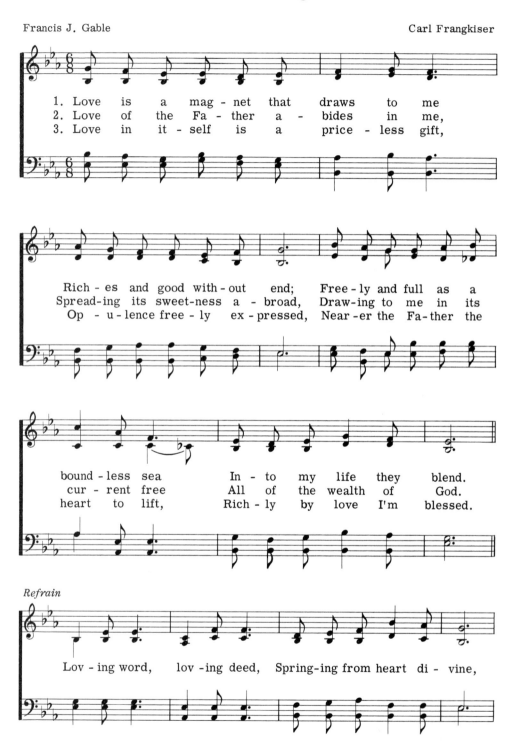

1. Love is a mag - net that draws to me
   Rich - es and good with - out end; Free - ly and full as a
   bound - less sea In - to my life they blend.

2. Love of the Fa - ther a - bides in me,
   Spread-ing its sweet-ness a - broad, Draw-ing to me in its
   cur - rent free All of the wealth of God.

3. Love in it - self is a price - less gift,
   Op - u - lence free - ly ex - pressed, Near-er the Fa-ther the
   heart to lift, Rich - ly by love I'm blessed.

Refrain

Lov - ing word, lov - ing deed, Spring-ing from heart di - vine,

Love in me shall suc-ceed, Mak-ing a-bun-dance mine.

May the Blessing of God Rest upon You   174

Hazrat Inayat Khan

Puran Khan Bair

May the bless-ing of God rest up-on you, May His

peace a-bide with you, May His pres-ence il-

lu-mi-nate your heart, Now and for-ev-er-more.

Words and melody from the "Teacher's Dance Manual."
Used by permission of the Sufi Islamia Ruhaniat Society.

175   O the Love That Knows No End

Janet Bowser Manning
Refrain from Mary A. Lathbury

CHAUTAUQUA
William F. Sherwin

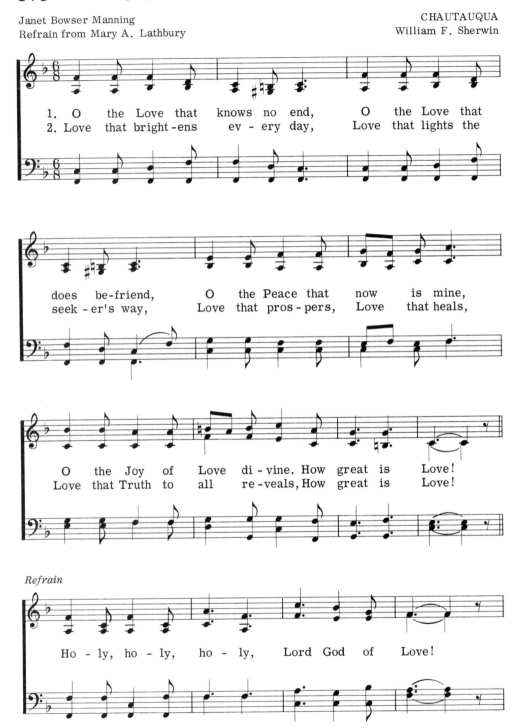

1. O the Love that knows no end, O the Love that
2. Love that bright-ens ev-ery day, Love that lights the

does be-friend, O the Peace that now is mine,
seek-er's way, Love that pros-pers, Love that heals,

O the Joy of Love di-vine. How great is Love!
Love that Truth to all re-veals, How great is Love!

Refrain

Ho - ly, ho - ly, ho - ly, Lord God of Love!

Heaven and earth are full of Thee, Heaven and earth are
prais - ing Thee, O Lord of Love!

God Is Good

176

DORRNANCE
Isaac B. Woodbury

Anonymous

1. God is good, the sky is say - ing; God is
(2. God is) love, the flowers are tell - ing; God is

great, the hills de - clare. 2. God is round us ev - ery - where.

177 The Love in Me

MEDITATION NO. 5

Dennis V. Connorton

G. Herald Keefer

The love in me be-holds the love in you.

The joy in me be-holds the joy in you.

The light in me be-holds the light in you.

We are one in the peace of the Lord! *(organ)* The Lord!

Lois J. Henrickson

Lois J. Henrickson
(Lytingale)

1. I am love, I am love. I am love, I am love. I am love, I am love, I am love. I am love, pure love.
2. I am light, I am light. I am light, I am light. I am light, I am light, I am light. I am light, pure light.
3. I am peace, I am peace. I am peace, I am peace. I am peace, I am peace, I am peace. I am peace, pure peace.
4. I am joy, I am joy. I am joy, I am joy. I am joy, I am joy, I am joy. I am joy, pure joy.
5. I am love, I am love. I am love, I am love. I am love, I am love, I am love. I am love, pure love.

179 Magic Penny

Malvina Reynolds   Malvina Reynolds

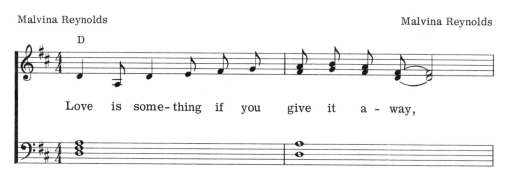

Love is some-thing if you give it a-way,

give it a-way, give it a-way. Love is some-thing if you

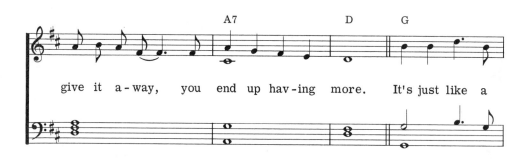

give it a-way, you end up hav-ing more. It's just like a

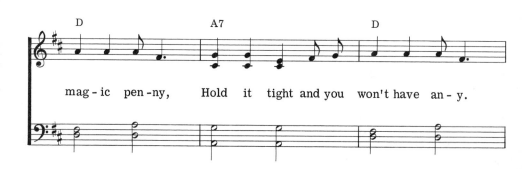

mag-ic pen-ny, Hold it tight and you won't have an-y.

180 Thou Art My Life

Clara H. Scott

Clara H. Scott

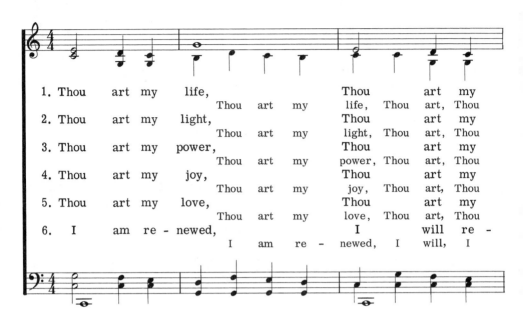

1. Thou art my life,   Thou art my
   Thou art my life, Thou art, Thou
2. Thou art my light,   Thou art my
   Thou art my light, Thou art, Thou
3. Thou art my power,   Thou art my
   Thou art my power, Thou art, Thou
4. Thou art my joy,   Thou art my
   Thou art my joy, Thou art, Thou
5. Thou art my love,   Thou art my
   Thou art my love, Thou art, Thou
6. I am re - newed,   I will re -
   I am re - newed, I will, I

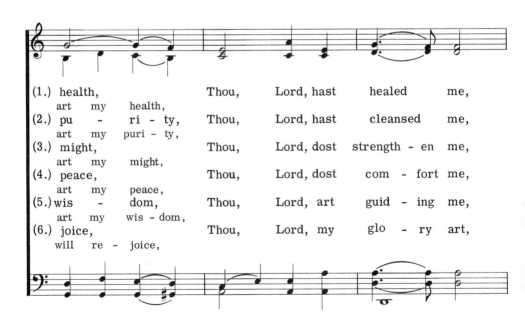

(1.) health,   Thou,   Lord, hast healed   me,
     art my health,
(2.) pu - ri - ty,   Thou,   Lord, hast cleansed   me,
     art my puri - ty,
(3.) might,   Thou,   Lord, dost strength - en me,
     art my might,
(4.) peace,   Thou,   Lord, dost com - fort me,
     art my peace,
(5.) wis - dom,   Thou,   Lord, art   guid - ing me,
     art my wis - dom,
(6.) joice,   Thou,   Lord, my   glo - ry art,
     will re - joice,

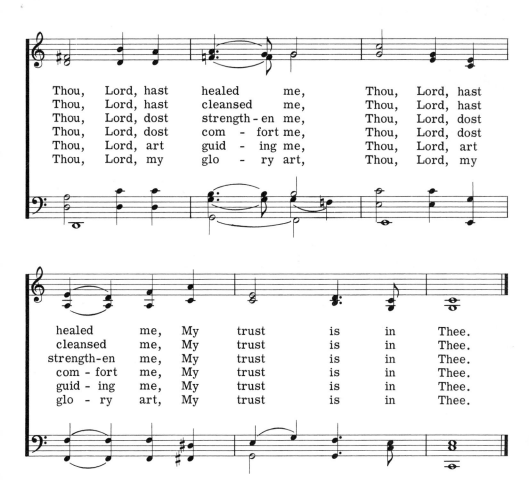

Thou, Lord, hast healed me, Thou, Lord, hast
Thou, Lord, hast cleansed me, Thou, Lord, hast
Thou, Lord, dost strength - en me, Thou, Lord, dost
Thou, Lord, dost com - fort me, Thou, Lord, dost
Thou, Lord, art guid - ing me, Thou, Lord, art
Thou, Lord, my glo - ry art, Thou, Lord, my

healed me, My trust is in Thee.
cleansed me, My trust is in Thee.
strength-en me, My trust is in Thee.
com - fort me, My trust is in Thee.
guid - ing me, My trust is in Thee.
glo - ry art, My trust is in Thee.

181 Breathe in Me, Breath of God

Edwin Hatch, adapted

NEW LIFE
J. B. Dick

1. Breathe in me, Breath of God, Fill me with life a - new, That I may love what Thou dost love, And do what Thou dost do.

2. Breathe in me, Breath of God, Un - til my heart is pure, Un - til with Thee I will one will, To do or to en - dure.

3. Breathe in me, Breath of God, Till I am whol - ly Thine, Till all this earth - ly part of me Glows with Thy fire di - vine.

4. Breathe in me, Breath of God, So shall I nev - er die, But live with Thee the per - fect life Of Thine e - ter - ni - ty.

The Joy of Living

182

JOY OF LIVING
Jonathan Hughes Arnett

Jonathan Hughes Arnett

1. I am the joy, the joy of liv-ing; It comes from giv-ing,
2. I am the joy, the joy of liv-ing; It comes from giv-ing,
3. I am the joy, the joy of liv-ing; It comes from giv-ing,

giv-ing, giv-ing. I give of love, I give of peace, I
giv-ing, giv-ing. I give of strength, I give of power, I
giv-ing, giv-ing. I give of hope, I give of cheer, I

give of joys that nev-er cease. I am the joy, the
give of joys for ev-ery hour. I am the joy, the
give of joys with-out a tear. I am the joy, the

joy of liv-ing; It comes from giv-ing, giv-ing, giv-ing.
joy of liv-ing; It comes from giv-ing, giv-ing, giv-ing.
joy of liv-ing; It comes from giv-ing, giv-ing, giv-ing.

183 I Am the Radiant Life of God

Georgiana Tree West
Hymnal version, 1984

RADIANT LIFE
Georgiana Tree West

1. I am the ra-di-ant life of God, I am, I am, I am, I am the radiant life of God, I am, I am, I am, I am, The health of God, the strength of God, Vi-tal-i-ty, en-er-gy, vim of God. I

2. I am the won-der-ful love of God, I am, I am, I am, I am the won-der-ful love of God, I am, I am, I am, I am, The peace of God, the joy of God, Se-ren-i-ty, har-mo-ny, rhythm of God. I

3. I am the wis-dom and power of God, I am, I am, I am, I am the wis-dom and power of God, I am, I am, I am, I am, The light of God, suc-cess of God, Pros-per-i-ty, hap-pi-ness, might of God. I

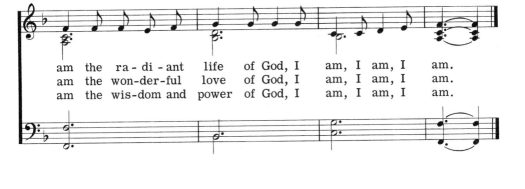

am the ra-di-ant life of God, I am, I am, I am.
am the won-der-ful love of God, I am, I am, I am.
am the wis-dom and power of God, I am, I am, I am.

I Am the Image of God

184

J. Sig Paulson
Janie Paulson

RADIANT LIFE
Georgiana Tree West

1. I am the image of God, I am,
       I am, I am, I am.
   I am the image of God, I am,
       I am, I am, I am.
   The image of love, of life, of health,
   The image of joy, of strength, of wealth,
   I am the image of God, I am,
       I am, I am, I am.

2. I am the image of God, I am,
       I am, I am, I am.
   I am the image of God, I am,
       I am, I am, I am.
   The image of good, of peace, of light,
   The image of Truth, of faith, of might,
   I am the image of God, I am,
       I am, I am, I am.

185 I'm the Expression of Infinite Life

An affirmation by
May Rowland

Irish Air

I'm the ev - er - re - new - ing, the ev - er - un - fold - ing ex -
pres - sion of in - fi - nite life. I'm the
ev - er - re - new - ing, the ev - er - un - fold - ing ex -
pres - sion of in - fi - nite life. The ex -

186 I Am God's Melody of Life

Georgiana Tree West

Georgiana Tree West
from a Scottish tune

I am God's mel - o - dy of life, He sings His song through me. I am God's rhythm and har - mo - ny, He sings His song through me. A song of life, Of ra - diant life, Of life so full and

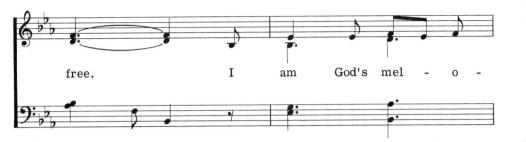

free.   I   am   God's mel - o -

dy   of life, *He   sings His song through me.

* The last two measures may be sung three times, gradually softer.

187 I'm Alive

Donald Curtis

Oman Ken
Arr. by ReBecca Oswald

I'm a-live with the joy of life, I'm in tune with the

song of life, I vi-brate with the en-er-gy of life,

I thrill to the beau-ty of life. I give thanks for the

gift of life, I'm a-lert to the chal-lenge of life, I

work at the ac - tiv-i-ty of life, I hap-pi-ly play the

game of life. And I cher-ish life. I re-

veal life, I love life, I live life. And I cher-ish life. And I

thank You, Fa-ther, for Your Life in my life.

188   O Life That Maketh All Things New

Samuel Longfellow, adapted
Refrain: Anonymous

THE SOLID ROCK
William B. Bradbury

1. O Life, that mak - eth all things new, The bloom - ing earth, the thoughts of men! Our pil - grim feet, wet with thy dew, In glad - ness hith - er turn a - gain.

2. From hand to hand the greet - ing flows; From eye to eye the sig - nals run; From heart to heart the bright faith glows; The seek - ers of the Light are one.

3. One in the free - dom of the Truth; One in the joy of paths un - trod; One in the soul's per - en - nial youth; One in the larg - er thought of God.

4. The fre - er step, the full - er love, The wide ho - ri - zon's grand - er view, The peace that com - eth from a - bove, The life that mak - eth all things new.

Refrain

U - nit - ed in the Truth we stand, Pro - claim - ing peace to

ev - ery land, Pro - claim-ing peace to ev - er - y land.

A Morning Song 189

G. Herald Keefer

G. Herald Keefer

1. Ear - ly in the morn-ing Let our prais-es rise. For we
2. Bless-ed Ho - ly Spir - it, Pour up - on us now. May we

bless You, thank You, praise You, Fa-ther of us all!
all re - ceive Your bless - ing, Fa-ther of us all!

Interlude

190 Wonderful Words of Life

Philip P. Bliss
Adapted by Christina Hovemann

WORDS OF LIFE
Philip P. Bliss

1. Sing them o-ver a-gain to me, Won-der-ful words of life; Let me more of their beau-ty see, Won-der-ful words of life. Words of life and beau-ty, Teach me faith and du-ty:
2. Words of prom-ise for all man-kind, Won-der-ful words of life; Bring-ing com-fort and peace of mind, Won-der-ful words of life. Prom-is-es to cheer me, Words I treas-ure dear-ly:
3. Words of wis-dom en-rich my soul, Won-der-ful words of life; Ev-er strength-en and make me whole, Won-der-ful words of life. Gems of wis-dom thrill-ing, Thirst for truth ful-fill-ing:

Refrain

Beau-ti-ful words,

won-der-ful words, Won-der-ful words of life;

Beau-ti-ful words, won-der-ful words, Won-der-ful words of life.

Sing the Glorious Words 191

WORDS OF LIFE
Philip P. Bliss

Ione G. Daniels

1. Sing the glorious words of Truth
   Over again to me,
   Let the light of eternal youth
   Breathe in their ecstasy.
   Words of health and beauty,
   Making joy of duty;

Refrain:
   Glorious words, beautiful words, Wonderful words of Truth!
   Glorious words, beautiful words, Wonderful words of Truth!

2. Word and Spirit united lead
   Into the heavenly mind;
   He who hungers shall surely feed,
   He who searches, find.
   Words of strength and power,
   Meet for every hour.

Refrain

192   Let's Celebrate Life

Janet Bowser Manning   Janet Bowser Manning

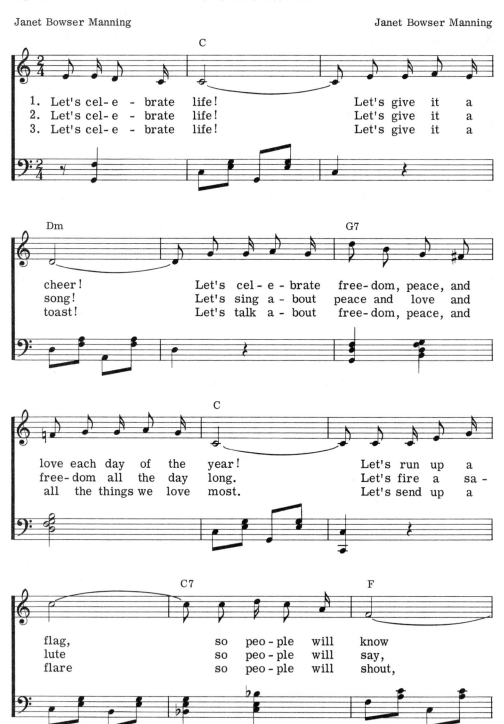

1. Let's cel-e-brate life!   Let's give it a
2. Let's cel-e-brate life!   Let's give it a
3. Let's cel-e-brate life!   Let's give it a

cheer!   Let's cel-e-brate free-dom, peace, and
song!   Let's sing a-bout peace and love and
toast!   Let's talk a-bout free-dom, peace, and

love each day of the year!   Let's run up a
free-dom all the day long.   Let's fire a sa-
all the things we love most.   Let's send up a

flag,   so peo-ple will know
lute   so peo-ple will say,
flare   so peo-ple will shout,

193   Festival of Life

Sharon Joy Backer   Sharon Joy Backer

1. Join in the fes-ti-val of life, let us sing.
2. Join in the fes-ti-val of life, let us dance.

Join in the fes-ti-val of life, let us sing.
Join in the fes-ti-val of life, let us dance.

Look to the Lord and you'll see His face, Then bring the joy to the
Dance to the rhythm of life's own song, Love will guide your

hu-man race. Sing to the glo-ry of the light with-in,
move-ment on. The spir-it of the Lord will lift you high,

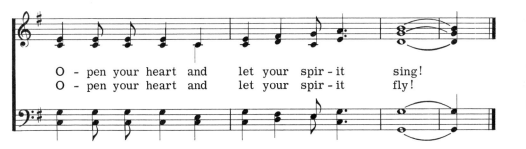

O - pen your heart and let your spir-it sing!
O - pen your heart and let your spir-it fly!

I'm One with God 194

George LeRoy Dale

Henry Tucker

1. I'm one with God, God's one with me; I'm
2. I'm one with love, it's one with me; I'm
3. I'm one with peace, it's one with me; I'm

one with God, God's one with me; I'm one with God, God's
one with love, it's one with me; I'm one with love, it's
one with peace, it's one with me; I'm one with peace, it's

one with me; I'm one with God, God's one with me.
one with me; I'm one with love, it's one with me.
one with me; I'm one with peace, it's one with me.

195 Life Is for Living

Carmen Moshier

Carmen Moshier

1. Life is for liv-ing; what-ev-er you will live for, you will give. Life is for giv-ing; what-ev-er you will give to life will live. Life is for do-ing;

2. Life is for lov-ing; what-ev-er you will love e-nough is yours. Life is for shar-ing; what-ev-er you will share with oth-ers grows. Life is for be-ing;

196 My Peace I Leave with Thee

Geraldine D. Robinson

JEWETT
Arr. from Carl Maria von Weber

1. "My peace I leave with thee." Thus soft-ly speaks the Son To ev-ery trou-bled heart, To ev-ery sor-row-ing one: "Not as the cold world gives, Give I this gift di-vine;

2. I come, O Christ, to Thee, The life, the Truth, the way; Thy yoke of serv-ice true Up-on my heart I lay. Teach Thou my will-ing soul The Truth of love su-preme,

3. No more shall doubt or fear Dis-turb my tran-quil breast; For Thou, O Christ, art here, And in the Truth I rest. Peace! Peace! sweet peace of Christ! O peace di-vine-ly free!

Come, rest with - in my love, And know this peace of mine!"
Till all un - rest and care Fade like a fleet- ing dream.
In - fold, per - vade me now And through e - ter - ni - ty.

Blest Be the Tie That Binds

197

DENNIS
Johann G. Nägeli
Arranged by Lowell Mason

John Fawcett

Blest be the tie that binds Our hearts in

Chris - tian love; The fel - low - ship of

kin - dred minds Is like to that a - bove.

198 Peace, Sweet Peace

Luther Lorentz

Luther Lorentz

1. There's a bless - ing for you and for
2. When I rest in this won - der - ful
3. I am pu - ri - fied, bod - y and

me So great that the eye can - not see; It
peace, All thoughts of the out - er world cease. I
soul; Through in - fi - nite Mind I'm made whole, I'm

comes as a to - ken of love and good will; 'Tis
dwell in the heav - en - ly king - dom of God Through
quick - ened and strength - ened; at last I am free Through

Refrain

peace, sweet peace.
peace, sweet peace. Peace, peace, sweet peace! I
peace, sweet peace.

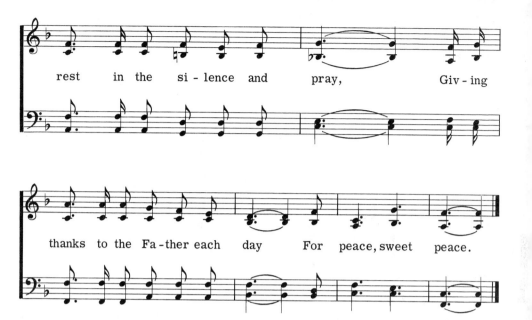

199 Like a River Glorious

Words adapted from
Frances R. Havergal

MERRIAL
Joseph Barnby

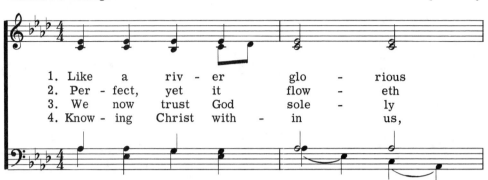

1. Like a riv - er glo - rious
2. Per - fect, yet it flow - eth
3. We now trust God sole - ly
4. Know - ing Christ with - in us,

Is God's per - fect peace, O - ver all vic -
Full - er ev - ery day; Per - fect, yet it
All through us to do; We who trust Him
Hearts are ful - ly blessed, Find - ing, as He

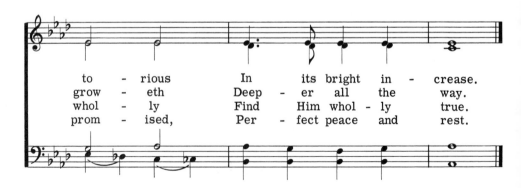

to - rious In its bright in - crease.
grow - eth Deep - er all the way.
whol - ly Find Him whol - ly true.
prom - ised, Per - fect peace and rest.

Peace I Have Most Full and Free

Corrie E. M. Hatcher

Abel Fiske

1. Peace I have most full and free,
   Peace from sim - ply trust-ing Thee;
   Joy se-rene I hold all day,
   When I fol - low Christ, the Way.

2. Love di - vine in - clud - ing all,
   From the great - est to the small,
   Can be mine in that de - gree
   That I let it shine through me.

3. Safe from fears am I and whole,
   Through the Christ with - in my soul;
   Rest I have in ev - ery-thing,
   When to Thee I close - ly cling.

4. Sat - is - fac - tion full, com - plete,
   Fills me with its fra-grance sweet;
   Health of bod - y and of mind
   In the liv - ing Christ I find.

201   Peace! Wonderful Peace

W. D. Cornell, alt.

WONDERFUL PEACE
W. G. Cooper

1. Far a-way in the depths of my spir-it to-night Rolls a mel-o-dy sweet-er than psalm; In ce-les-tial-like strains it un-ceas-ing-ly falls O'er my soul like an in-fi-nite calm.

2. What a treas-ure I have in this won-der-ful peace, Bur-ied deep in the heart of my soul; So se-cure that no pow-er can mine it a-way While the years of e-ter-ni-ty roll.

3. I am rest-ing to-night in this won-der-ful peace, Rest-ing sweet-ly in Je-sus' con-trol; For I'm kept from all dan-ger by night and by day, And His glo-ry is flood-ing my soul.

Refrain

Peace! peace! won-der-ful peace, Com-ing down from the Fa-ther a-

bove; Sweep o - ver my spir - it for -

ev - er, I pray, In fath - om - less bil - lows of love.

Vesper Hymn 202

Samuel Longfellow, excerpt

Adapted from VESPER HYMN
Russian Air

Ju - bi - la - te! Ju - bi - la - te! Ju - bi - la - te! A - men!

1. Sweet - ly let us join in sing - ing; Ju - bi - la - te! A - men!
2. Now the ves - per hymn is ring - ing; Ju - bi - la - te! A - men!

203 What a Fellowship

SHOWALTER

Elisha A. Hoffman

Anthony J. Showalter

1. What a fel - low-ship, what a joy di - vine,
2. O how sweet to walk in this pil - grim way,
3. What have I to dread? What have I to fear?

Lean - ing on the ev - er - last - ing arms;
Lean - ing on the ev - er - last - ing arms;
Lean - ing on the ev - er - last - ing arms;

What a bless - ed - ness, what a peace is mine,
O how bright the path grows from day to day,
I have bless - ed peace with my Lord so near,

Lean - ing on the ev - er - last - ing arms.
Lean - ing on the ev - er - last - ing arms.
Lean - ing on the ev - er - last - ing arms.

204   Thou Wilt Keep Him in Perfect Peace

PERFECT PEACE
Vivian Kretz

Vivian Kretz

"Thou wilt keep him in per-fect peace whose mind is stayed on Thee." When the shad-ows come and dark-ness falls, He giv-eth in-ward peace. O He is the on-ly per-fect rest-ing place, He giv-eth per-fect peace! "Thou wilt keep him in per-fect peace whose mind is stayed on Thee."

Peace Like a River

Mrs. M. W. Carr

Charles K. Langley

1. Peace like a riv - er, It flow - eth so free,
2. Peace like a riv - er To him who be - lieves,
3. Peace like a riv - er, It flow - eth al - way,

Out from the heart of In - fin - i - ty,
Peace to the heart that the Sav - iour re - ceives,
Mak - ing the dark - ness as fair as the day.

O bless - ed spir - it, It flow - eth for thee,
Peace to the spir - it That sor - rows and grieves,
Peace like a riv - er, O wea - ry one, pray For

Peace like a riv-er, Peace like a riv-er.
Peace like a riv-er, Peace like a riv-er.
Peace like a riv-er, Peace like a riv-er.

206 This Is My Song

Lloyd Stone
Stanza 3, Georgia Harkness

FINLANDIA
Jean Sibelius
Arr. for *The Hymnal*, 1933

1. This is my song, O God of all the na-tions,
2. My coun-try's skies are blu-er than the o-cean,
3. This is my prayer, O Lord of all earth's king-doms,

A song of peace for lands a-far and mine.
And sun-light beams on clo-ver-leaf and pine.
Thy king-dom come; on earth Thy will be done.

This is my home, the coun-try where my heart is;
But oth-er lands have sun-light too, and clo-ver,
Let Christ be lift-ed up till all men serve Him,

Here are my hopes, my dreams, my ho-ly shrine;
And skies are ev-ery-where as blue as mine.
And hearts u-nit-ed learn to live as one.

But oth-er hearts in oth-er lands are beat-ing
Oh, hear my song, Thou God of all the na-tions,
Oh, hear my prayer, Thou God of all the na-tions.

With hopes and dreams as true and high as mine.
A song of peace for their land and for mine.
My-self I give Thee; let Thy will be done.

207 O Brother Man

O PERFECT LOVE

John Greenleaf Whittier

Joseph Barnby

1. O broth-er man, fold to thy heart thy broth-er;
2. Fol-low with rev-erent steps the great ex-am-ple
3. Then shall all shack-les fall; the storm-y clang-or

Where kind-ness dwells, the peace of God is there;
Of Him whose ho-ly work was do-ing good:
Of wild war mu-sic o'er the earth shall cease;

To wor-ship right-ly is to love each oth-er,
So shall the wide earth seem our Fa-ther's tem-ple,
Love shall tread out the bale-ful fire of an-ger,

Each smile a hymn, each kind-ly deed a prayer.
Each lov-ing life a psalm of grat-i-tude.
And in its ash-es plant the tree of peace.

We Sing the New Religion

AURELIA
Samuel S. Wesley

Ella Wheeler Wilcox, adapted

1. We sing the new re - li - gion, the fel-low-ship of man;
2. The path-way to sal - va - tion seek not in realms a - bove;
3. A - wake, O soul im - mor - tal! and find the God with - in;

We sing the new trans - la - tion of God's pri - me - val plan;
It lies di - rect be - fore you, the guide-posts name it Love;
This earth is heaven's own por - tal and an - gels are your kin;

Su - prem - a - cy of good - ness, and love's tri - um-phant strain,
Re - joice in will - ing serv - ice; who loves will la - bor best,
No fa - bled fall of Ad - am can chain you to the sod;

The sav - ing grace of beau - ty, all these are our re - frain.
You are your own Re - deem - er, in His pure love you're blessed.
You are the child of Glo - ry, the mes - sen - ger of God.

Used with the permission of First Divine Science Church of Denver.

209   Let There Be Unity

Gloria McGill

Gloria McGill

Arr. by Harriet Haner

Let there be u-ni-ty in all the world to-day. Let it be known that God a-lone can show the way. Let there be Truth in all the hearts of men, for Truth will make them free. Let there be peace on earth and let it be-gin with

210 A Family of Love

Carmen Moshier

Carmen Moshier

Medium tempo

We work to-geth-er (that's the way), We work to-geth-er as we say: "We're a fam-i-ly, we're a fam-i-ly, We're a fam-i-ly of love." We play to-geth-er (that's the way), We play to-geth-er as we say: "We're a fam-i-ly, we're a fam-i-ly, We're a fam-i-ly of love."

1. We
2. Our

211 Oneness

Carmen Moshier

Carmen Moshier

1. I now let go, there's noth-ing to fear. I now let go, there's noth-ing to fear. I now let go, there's noth-ing to fear.
2. I re-al-ize there's on-ly one power. I re-al-ize there's on-ly one power. I re-al-ize there's on-ly one power.
3. I re-al-ize, I'm one with the One. I re-al-ize, I'm one with the One. I re-al-ize, I'm one with the One.

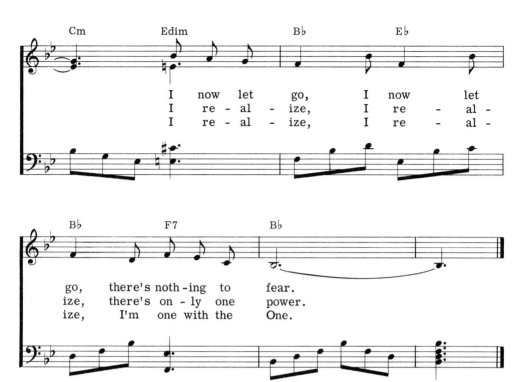

I   now   let   go,   I   now   let
I   re - al - ize,   I   re - al -
I   re - al - ize,   I   re - al -

go,   there's noth -ing to   fear.
ize,   there's on - ly one   power.
ize,   I'm   one with the   One.

212 Weave

Rosemary Crow

Rosemary Crow

Moderato
Refrain

Weave, weave, weave us to-geth-er.

Weave us to-geth-er in u-ni-ty and love.

Weave, weave, weave us to-geth-er.

Weave us to-geth-er, to-geth-er in love.

213

What Is Unity?

Carmen Moshier   Carmen Moshier

1. Oh, what is u - ni - ty? That means we're one,
2. Oh, what is peace on earth? Not some - thing won!

We're one with ev - ery-thing and ev - ery - one.
Al - read - y here in us since time be - gun.

But we must know that we're in u - ni - ty,
But I must know that peace be - gins with me,

And we must live as one for it to be.
And I must show that peace is mine to be!

214 Brethren in Peace Together

Jewish Folk Song
Psalm 133:1, paraphrased

Jewish Folk Song

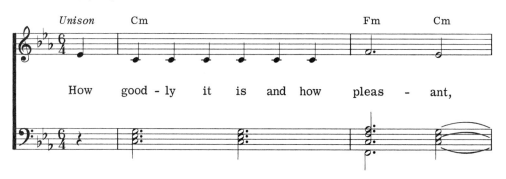

How good-ly it is and how pleas - ant,

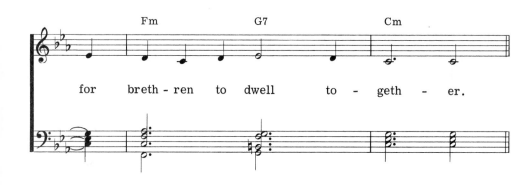

for breth - ren to dwell to - geth - er.

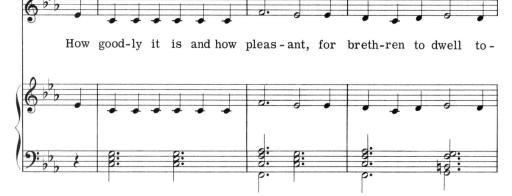

How good-ly it is and how pleas - ant, for breth-ren to dwell to-

To sing as a round, Group 2 should enter at I. when Group 1 reaches II.

II.

geth - er. Good - ly, pleas - ant,

Breth-ren in peace to - geth - er. How good-ly it is and how

pleas - ant, for breth -ren to dwell to - geth - er.

(To finish as a round, repeat last four
measures – omit upper notes.)

215   The Father and I Are One

Traditional

Aloha Oe

Adapted version from
Unity in Song

Queen Liliuokalani

1. A - lo - ha oe, A - lo - ha oe, E ke
2. We merge with life; we merge with joy; We

o - na - o - na no - ho i - ka li - po; One
merge with u - ni - ver - sal love and wis - dom; We

fond em - brace, a - ho - i a - e au, Un -
merge with light; We merge with all man - kind, And

til we meet a - gain.
live in peace on earth.

217 One with Him Whose Matchless Power

Elizabeth J. Moyer

EBENEZER
Thomas J. Williams

1. One with Him whose match - less pow - er
2. Be ye per - fect as the Fa - ther,

Guides His worlds through bound - less space;
With Christ's life your life im - bue;

One with Him whose love un - meas - ured
"Bide with me," so saith the Mas - ter,

Kin - dles hope in ev - ery race.
"That my words may live in you."

Music used by permission of Dilys Evans and Eluned Crump.

One with Thee, O gra - cious Fa - ther,
In this realm of Truth and Spir - it,

One with Christ, Thine own dear Son;
Wis - dom, pow - er, love un - told

One in thought and as - pi - ra - tion.
Mold our thoughts and guide our foot - steps.

On - ly thus Thy will is done.
Peace and joy our lives in - fold.

218

Unity

Francis J. Gable

UNITY
Edna Gieselman

Tempo di marcia

1. We fol - low Christ the U - ni - ty way, The
2. The time we spend in U - ni - ty thought Brings
3. The prayer of faith is U - ni - ty's prayer, To
4. It's joy to feel the U - ni - ty bond, At
5. We glo - ry in our U - ni - ty growth In

way of stud - y and prayer, When help we need, to
joy and bless-ing to all, We think the thought, we
bless, to pros - per, to heal; As we be - lieve, it
one with Fa - ther and Son, For when we find the
bod - y, spir - it, and soul, To see the Christ in

Him we turn, And find Him al - ways there.
speak the word, And God heeds ev - ery call.
does its work, His pres - ence to re - veal.
Christ with - in, His per - fect work is done.
ev - ery one—That makes us well and whole.

219   We Are Workers All

Francis J. Gable

UNITY
Edna Gieselman

Unison

1. We're work - ers all at U - ni - ty School, We
2. The work we do at U - ni - ty School Means

love to laugh and to grow; We live to learn, we
joy and peace to all; We think the thought, we

learn to live, To spread the Truth we know.
speak the word, And God heeds ev - ery call.

Refrain

U - N - I - T - Y, U - NI - TY, We've

found the Truth that makes us free! We

send you a mes - sage of Truth, light, and love, We're

hap - py folks at U - NI - TY.

220 New Mercies, New Blessings

ADESTE FIDELES
Frances R. Havergal, adapted
John F. Wade, *Cantus Diversi*

1. New mer - cies, new bless - ings, new light on thy
2. New wine in thy chal - ice, new al - tars to
3. New stars for thy crown and new to - kens of

way; New cour - age, new hope, and new
raise; New fruits for thy Mas - ter, new
love; New gleams of the glo - ry that

strength for each day; New notes of thanks - giv - ing, new
gar - ments of praise; New gifts from His treas - ures, new
shines from a - bove; New light on thy path - way,

chords of de - light; New praise in the
smiles from His face; New streams from the
full and un - priced; All this be the

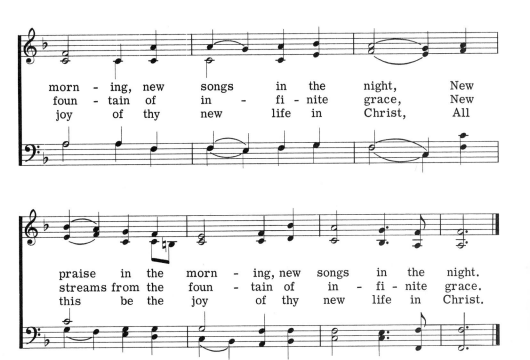

morn - ing, new songs in the night, New
foun - tain of in - fi - nite grace, New
joy of thy new life in Christ, All

praise in the morn - ing, new songs in the night.
streams from the foun - tain of in - fi - nite grace.
this be the joy of thy new life in Christ.

221 It's a Special Day

Warren Meyer

MINOR
George A. Minor

1. Some-thing is oc-cur-ring; Some-thing new is stir-ring;
2. Knowl-edge is pro-vid-ed; I am be-ing guid-ed;
3. I ac-cept my bless-ing; Through it I'm ex-press-ing

Some-thing of the Spir-it Bless-es me to-day.
Some-thing of the Spir-it Bless-es me with light.
Some-thing of the Spir-it Glo-ri-ous-ly good.

En-er-gies are swarm-ing, To-tal-ly trans-form-ing;
I have per-fect lead-ing To the good I'm need-ing;
Ev-ery trou-ble ceas-es; All my joy in-creas-es;

Some-thing of the Spir-it Bless-es me to-day.
Some-thing of the Spir-it Bless-es me with light.
Some-thing of the Spir-it Bless-es me with good.

Refrain

It's a spe - cial day! It's a spe - cial day!

I can feel it deep - ly in a spe - cial way.

It's a spe - cial day! It's a spe - cial day!

I can feel it deep - ly in a spe - cial way.

222   My Life Begins for Me Today

Frank B. Whitney

ELLACOMBE
Gesangbuch, Wirtemberg, 1784

1. My life be - gins for me to - day! New
2. To - day for me be - gins a - new A

worlds be - fore me lie! The yes - ter - days have
life that holds for me All that is good and

passed a - way, No more to cause a sigh. Be -
real and true, It's bless - ings now I see. I

fore me lies the bright to - day, All
look no long - er to the past, Nor

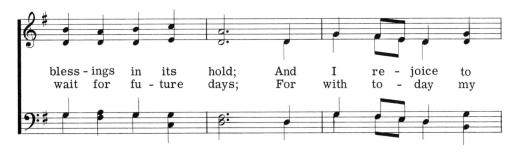

bless - ings in its hold; And I re - joice to
wait for fu - ture days; For with to - day my

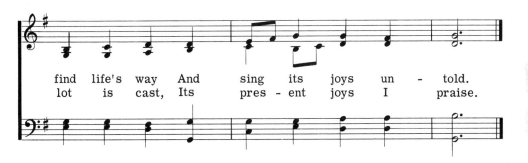

find life's way And sing its joys un - told.
lot is cast, Its pres - ent joys I praise.

Awake! Awake!   223

ELLACOMBE
Gesangbuch, Wirtemberg, 1784

McCardell

1. Awake! Awake! Ye souls, awake!
   The hour has come at last;
   The morning hour, when light doth break,
   Through ages overcast.
   Arise, seek God, and ye shall find
   Truths that to few are given;
   Teach them with care and love combined,
   And make this earth as heaven.

224 New Horizons

Eric Butterworth

Eric Butterworth

New ho - ri-zons out be-fore our view,
Reach - ing for-ward, claim-ing all things new. We've
caught the loft-y vi-sion of God's pres-ence ev- er - where. We
turn our backs on past mis-takes and find re-lease through prayer.

225   New Horizons

Bill Provost
Based on poem by Eric Butterworth

Bill Provost

1. New ho - ri - zons out be - fore our
2. New ho - ri - zons we are sure to

view;   God   is   bless - ing me and
find   In   our   pres - ent state of

you.   There are cas - tles
mind.   And with Christ to

in the air,   Dreams that we can share;
show the way,

226   Let's Be

Carmen Moshier   Carmen Moshier

Let's be what we're made to be; Is-n't this our des-ti-ny?

Let's get start-ed now to-day, Up-ward on our way.

Let's be what we real-ly are, Seek and find our in-ner star.

Let's go for-ward in the light, Fac-es shin-ing bright.

Sons of God, un - lim-it - ed are we,

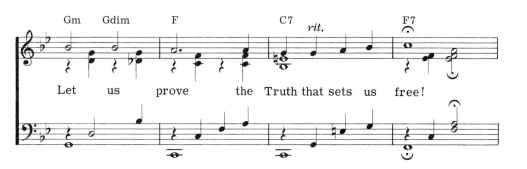

Let us prove the Truth that sets us free!

Let's ac-cept our high-est good, Know-ing we're in broth-er-hood.

Now the good in all we see. Let's don't wait, let's be!

For emphasis, repeat this page.

227   New Age Vision

BATTLE HYMN OF THE REPUBLIC

Henry Victor Morgan, adapted   William Steffe

1. Mine eyes have seen the com - ing Of an age that is to be, When from ev - ery lim - i - ta - tion I shall know that I am free; For the age is rich in prom - ise And my soul has eyes to see God's Truth is march - ing on.

2. My soul has seen the beau - ty Of a race from sor - row free, An age of faith and jus - tice, Truth and love and lib - er - ty; And I sing of love's great tri - umph In this time of ju - bi - lee. God's Truth is march - ing on.

3. I have seen the free - born wom - an Stand - ing side by side with man. I have seen the na - tions broad - en Till there is no tribe or clan, And the war - lords all have van - ished In the love of man for man. God's Truth is march - ing on.

Words from "Hymns of Health and Gladness."
Used by permission of Murray Morgan and Victor Morgan.

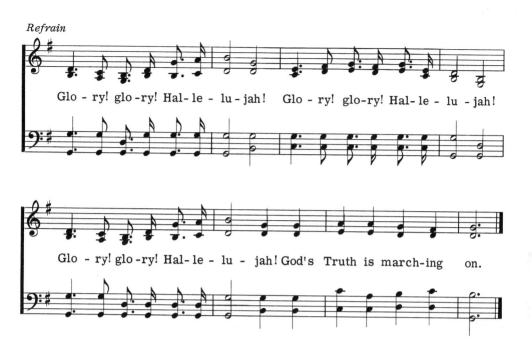

Glo - ry! glo -ry! Hal- le - lu -jah! Glo - ry! glo-ry! Hal- le - lu - jah!

Glo - ry! glo -ry! Hal- le - lu - jah! God's Truth is march-ing on.

228 A Golden Dawn Is Breaking

Christina Hovemann

LANCASHIRE
Henry Smart

1. A gold-en dawn is break-ing, The shades of night will
2. The gold-en day is dawn-ing, And light of Truth ap-
3. The gold-en day ad-vanc-ing Now sheds a won-drous

flee, And sons of men a-wak-ing, The
pears, The first bright ray of morn-ing Dis-
light, And rays of Truth en-hanc-ing Make

light of Truth shall see. We hail its light with
pels our dark-est fears. With peace and lov-ing-
all things pure and bright; The sons of men, be-

glad-ness, Our hearts burst in-to song, For
kind-ness Trans-form-ing ev-ery heart, The
hold-ing, Find great-er goals to win, For

Truth will con-quer sad - ness, And joy shall reign ere long.
day of joy and glad - ness Shall nev - er - more de - part.
now we see un - fold - ing, The light of God with - in!

Another Year   229

LANCASHIRE
Henry Smart

Frances R. Havergal, adapted

1. Another year is dawning!
   Dear Master, it shall be,
   In working or in waiting,
   Another year with Thee.
   Another year of progress;
   Another year of praise;
   Another year of proving
   Thy presence "all the days."

2. Another year of mercies,
   Of faithfulness and grace;
   Another year of gladness
   In shining of Thy face;
   Another year is dawning!
   Dear Master, it shall be,
   In working or in waiting,
   Another year with Thee.

230   We Hail the Dawning of the Day

HAIL THE DAWNING

Elisha A. Hoffman, alt.

Elisha A. Hoffman

1. We hail the dawn - ing of the day, For the king - dom of Christ is come; Where Love and Truth now have full sway, For the king - dom of Christ is come; Now to the earth's re - mot - est bound The

2. The reign of peace shall be com - plete, For the king - dom of Christ is come; The earth shall bow at Je - sus' feet, For the king - dom of Christ is come; For - ev - er shouts of joy re - sound, For

gos - pel mes - sage does re - sound, And peace and sweet good
peace and plen - ty shall a - bound, And broth - er - hood and

will a - bound, For the king - dom of Christ is come.
love pro - found, For the king - dom of Christ is come.

Refrain

For the king - dom is come, For the king - dom is come, O

this is now a joy - ous time, For the king - dom of Christ is come!

231 Let's Begin

Bill Provost   Bill Provost

With feeling

Let's be-gin from this mo-ment; Let's be-gin now.

2nd time to Coda ⊕

From with-in feel ex-cite-ment to be-gin now.

To grow as we fol-low the

thread of life, shar-ing love with the bread of life,

mak-ing all things new. To know,

232   I Am the Light of the World

Jim Strathdee   Jim Strathdee

"I am the light of the world!

You peo-ple come and fol-low me!" If you

fol-low and love You'll learn the mys-ter-y of

what you were meant to do and be.

233 This Is the Year

Russell A. Kemp

Bill Provost

Joyfully

1. Won - der -ful, won - der -ful, for - tu - nate you,
2. This is the year when you know the Truth;

This is the year that your dreams come true!
This is the year when you find new youth.

This is the year that your ship comes in;
This is the year that brings hap - pi - ness;

1.

This is the year you find Christ with - in.
This is the year you will

234

This Is the Year

Russell A. Kemp, adapted

Warren Meyer

1. Won-der-ful, won-der-ful, for-tu-nate you,
2. This is the year you will be glad to live;
3. This is the year that will bring hap-pi-ness;

This is the year that your dreams come true!
This is the year you have much to give.
This is the year you will live to bless.

This is the year that your ships come in;
This is the year when you know the Truth;
Won-der-ful, won-der-ful, for-tu-nate you,

This is the year you find Christ with-in.
This is the year when you find new youth.
This is the year that your dreams come true!

Music used by permission.

Purer in Heart, O God

Anna L. Davison, adapted

J. H. Fillmore

1. Pur - er in heart, O God, Help me to be;
2. Pur - er in heart, O God, Help me to be;
3. Pur - er in heart, O God, Help me to be;

May I de - vote my life Whol - ly to Thee.
Teach me to do Thy will Most lov - ing - ly.
That I Thy ho - ly face Each day may see.

Lead Thou my ea - ger feet, Guide me with coun-sel sweet;
Be Thou my Friend and Guide, Let me with Thee a - bide;
Reign Thou with - in my soul; Keep me, Lord, free and whole;

Pur - er in heart Help me to be.
Pur - er in heart Help me to be.
Pur - er in heart Help me to be.

236   Take My Life and Let It Be

CONCONE

Frances R. Havergal   Arranged from G. Concone

1. Take my life, and let it be Con - se - crat - ed, Lord, to Thee; Take my mo - ments and my days; Let them flow in cease-less praise.
2. Take my voice, and let me sing Al - ways, on - ly, for my King; Take my lips, and let them be Filled with mes - sag - es from Thee.
3. Take my will, and make it Thine; It shall be no long - er mine; Take my heart, it is Thine own; It shall be Thy roy - al throne.

Take my hands, and let them move At the
Take my sil - ver and my gold; Not a
Take my love; my Lord, I pour At Thy

im - pulse of Thy love; Take my feet, and
mite would I with - hold; Take my in - tel -
feet its treas - ure store; Take my - self, and

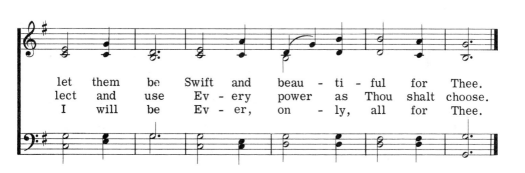

let them be Swift and beau - ti - ful for Thee.
lect and use Ev - ery power as Thou shalt choose.
I will be Ev - er, on - ly, all for Thee.

237 The Gospel in One Word Is Love

Spiritual Dancing

Traditional

Love, love, love, love, The gos-pel in one word is love;

Love thy neigh-bor as thy-self, Love, love, love.

238 Truth Will Lift Me

LIFE STREAM OF GOD

Francis J. Gable

Carl Frangkiser

Truth will lift me, Truth will free me If I

o - pen wide my heart. Let its sooth - ing pres - ence

heal me, Let it fill its per - fect part.

Refrain

The life stream of God now flows through me; It

quick-ens, it strength-ens, it makes me free. No pow-er so cleans-ing can

ev - er be. Lord, I yield to Thee.

Thou Wilt Keep Him in Perfect Peace

from Pluma M. Brown

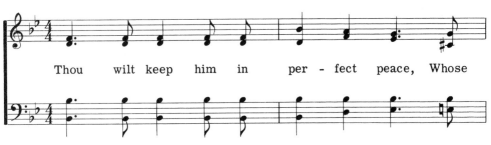

Thou wilt keep him in per - fect peace, Whose

mind is stayed on Thee.

240

The Chant of the Ongoers

Frank B. Whitney

Carl Frangkiser

1. They walk up - on il - lu - mined paths, a pag-eant - ry of
2. To them there is no e - vil nigh, these chant-ers of the
3. And so these sons of light press on, and for-ward, up-ward,

light; They chant the song of men made free, they
good; To them naught but the good ex - ists, for
go; They sing their song: "God is! I am! I

sing of health and might. Now, in the great on -
God is un - der - stood. And in the great on -
love! I see! I know!" And in the great on -

go - ing there can be no note of fear, For
go - ing there are nev - er e - vil things, For
go - ing God and man are one some - how; For

on - ly God as love ex - ists; to them as love He's near.
on - ly God as good ex - ists; of Him the chant - er sings.
man with God, the One, ex - ists; as God with man, here, now.

241 The Greatest Thing

Mark Pendergrass

Mark Pendergrass

The great-est thing in all my life is

1. know - ing
2. lov - ing You.
3. serv - ing

The great-est thing in all my life is

know - ing
lov - ing You.
serv - ing

I want to

242 Just Where Thou Art

Elisha A. Hoffman

Elisha A. Hoffman

1. Just where thou art, lift up thy voice, And in the
2. Just where thou stand-est, let thy light Shine forth for
3. Just where thou art, be brave and true; Keep God and
4. Some paths may seem more fair and bright, Some lives more

Sav - iour's love re - joice; Sing out the song that stirs the
Je - sus, clear and bright; This is thy soul's ap - point-ed
right and heaven in view; Al - ways a - lert to do thy
lu - mi - nous with light; Serve thou the Lord with voice and

heart, And live for God just where thou art.
part, To be a light just where thou art.
part; Be brave and true just where thou art.
heart, Not some-where else, but where thou art.

Refrain

Just where thou art, shine forth and glow; Just where thou

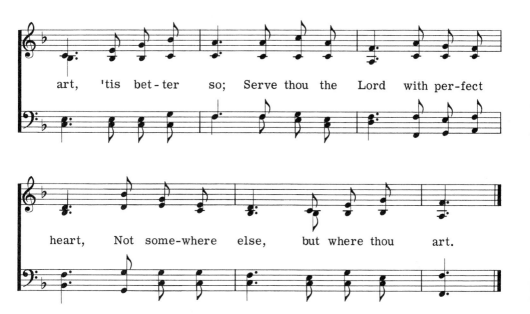

art, 'tis bet-ter so; Serve thou the Lord with per-fect

heart, Not some-where else, but where thou art.

243   I Would Be True

PEEK

Howard A. Walter, adapted

Joseph Y. Peek

1. I would be true, for there are those who trust me;
2. I would be friend of all—the foe, the friend-less;

I would be pure, for there are those who care;
I would be giv - ing, and for - get the gift;

I would be strong, for there are those who suf - fer;
I would be gen - tle, that I may bless oth - ers;

I would be brave, for there is much to dare,
I would look up, and laugh, and love, and lift,

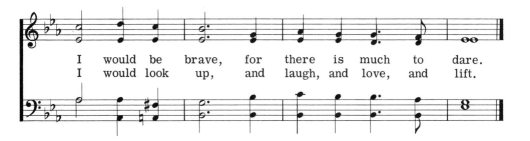

I would be brave, for there is much to dare.
I would look up, and laugh, and love, and lift.

Affirmation 244

Vivian Yeiser Laramore   Henrietta Dippman Griswold

1. My mind shall mir - ror on - ly Truth, My
2. Through - out my be - ing love shall flow; The
3. My spo - ken word shall po - tent be To

bod - y pic - ture ra - diant youth, My heart - beat be a
cos - mic call my soul shall know; Ex - ult - ant, ea - ger,
bring my pre - cious own to me; Nor crowd, nor creed, nor

psalm of praise, My foot - steps paths of beau - ty blaze.
I shall claim The her - it - age for which I came.
seem - ing strife Shall keep me from the Source of life.

245

Awake, My Soul

Elinor Hiscock

TALLIS' CANON
Thomas Tallis

1. A - wake, my soul, to high - er thought! The
2. A - rise, my soul! cast off thy gloom; There
3. Stand up, my soul! thy birth - right claim; A
4. Go forth, my soul, to no - bler deed; A -

things of Truth can - not be bought; That which is real comes
is no night, there is no tomb; For all is light, and
child of God, be - hold thy name! Be - hind thee stands Om -
long the path of du - ty speed; For beau - ti - ful the

rich and free, If we but lift our souls to see.
all is life, And all is end - less joy, not strife.
nip - o - tence, Who works through thee; a - rise, go hence.
feet of those Which ti - dings good doth bring to foes.

Breathe Through Me

Marguerite Meyer   Warren Meyer

1. Breathe through me; breathe through me; O bless-ed
2. Live through me; live through me; O bless-ed
3. Speak through me; speak through me; O bless-ed

Spir - it, breathe through me. Breathe through me;
Spir - it, live through me. Live through me;
Spir - it, speak through me. Speak through me;

breathe through me; O bless-ed Spir - it, breathe through me.
live through me; O bless-ed Spir - it, live through me.
speak through me; O bless-ed Spir - it, speak through me.

4. Think through me . . .
5. Feel through me . . .
6. Sing through me . . .

247   Onward, Ever Onward

ST. GERTRUDE

Henry Victor Morgan, alt.   Arthur S. Sullivan

1. On - ward, ev - er on - ward, March-ing ev - er - more,
2. Like the change-less o - cean Is the Truth of God;
3. On - ward, ev - er on - ward, Till all men are free.

With Love's heal-ing mes - sage Ev - er to the fore;
Up - ward we are tread - ing Where the Christ has trod.
We shall see faith tri - umph, Love's great ju - bi - lee;

Truth our on - ly stand - ard, We can have no foe.
Ours the hope e - ter - nal, All God's seas to sail;
Glo - ry in the high - est Un - to Christ with - in;

For - ward, ev - er for - ward, See Love's ban - ner go.
Ours the faith su - per - nal That can nev - er fail.
This through count-less a - ges Is the song we sing.

Words from "Hymns of Health and Gladness."
Used by permission of Murray Morgan and Victor Morgan.

On-ward, ev-er on-ward, March-ing ev-er-more, With Love's heal-ing mes-sage Ev-er to the fore.

No Other Way 248

Could we but see the pattern of our days,
We should discern how devious were the ways
By which we came to this, the present time,
This place in life; and we should see the climb
Our soul has made up through the years.
We should forget the hurts, the wanderings, the fears,
The wastelands of our life, and know
That we could come no other way or grow
Into our good without these steps our feet
Found hard to take, our faith found hard to meet.
The road of life winds on, and we like travelers go
From turn to turn until we come to know
The truth that life is endless and that we
Forever are inhabitants of all eternity.

—*Martha Smock*

249   With a Perfect Heart

Helen L. Manning
Stanza 3, Ruth Bruner

PERFECT HEART
Ward Rockwell

1. Per - fect is my heart be - fore Thee, Per - fect walk I
2. Per - fect free - dom! I de - clare it! For the Truth has
3. Per - fect is Thy power, I feel it; Full - er life is

in Thy ways; Per - fect love e'en now re - stores me,
made me free. Per - fect peace! yea, naught shall mar it,
now in store. Christ in me, my hope of glo - ry;

Refrain

Per - fect is my song of praise.
For my mind is stayed on Thee.   I will walk with a
Praise Thy name for - ev - er - more!

per - fect heart, Love has cast out fear;

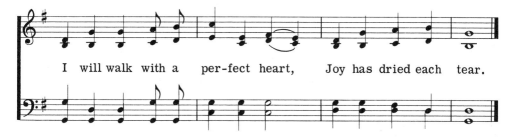

I will walk with a per-fect heart, Joy has dried each tear.

Walking Is a Prayer

250

Oman Ken
Arr. by ReBecca Oswald

J. Sig Paulson

Walk-ing is a prayer, Walk-ing is a prayer,

It's not hard to talk with Him

When I'm walk - ing in His gar - den.

For additional verses, use "Singing," "Dancing," etc.

251 Flow, Spirit, Flow

Janet Bowser Manning

Maori Folk Melody

1. Flow, Spir - it, flow, and all my fears re-
2. Heal, Spir - it, heal, and all my self re-

lease, I am a chan - nel
new. I am ex - press - ing

for Thy love and peace. Fill me with power
my per - fec - tion true. Fill me with love

and let my heart be strong. Fill
that I may lov - ing be. Fill

me with joy that I may sing Thy song.
me with life that I may live for Thee.

Thy Will, O Lord, Not Mine, Be Done 252

MORNING SONG

Herbert J. Hunt

Wyeth's *Repository of Sacred Music*, 1813
Harm. by Austin C. Lovelace

Unison

1. "Thy will, O Lord, not mine, be done!" This is my ear-nest prayer. My life, my all, I glad-ly place With-in His love and care. My life, my all, I glad-ly place With-in His love and care.

2. I have no fear! What-e'er be-tide, I'll trust the Fa-ther-hood! He leads me gen-tly, day by day, Un-to my high-est good. He leads me gen-tly, day by day, Un-to my high-est good.

3. The good I seek shall come to me In God's own won-drous way; The full-ness of His love is mine, And that a-bides al-way! The full-ness of His love is mine, And that a-bides al-way!

253

I Accept

Warren Meyer

PLEYEL'S HYMN (adapted)
Arranged from Ignace J. Pleyel

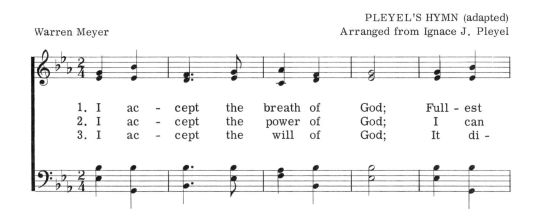

1. I ac - cept the breath of God; Full - est
2. I ac - cept the power of God; I can
3. I ac - cept the will of God; It di -

life I find. I ac - cept the
do all things. I ac - cept the
rects my way. I ac - cept the

light of God; It re - news my mind.
love of God; All my be - ing sings.
peace of God; How se - rene I stay.

O Christ, Thou Son of God

254

PICARDY, adapted
Melody based on a French Carol

Unknown

Unison

O Christ, Thou Son of God, My own e - ter - nal Self, Live Thou Thy life in me, Live Thou Thy love in me, Do Thou Thy will in me, Be Thou made flesh in me, I will have no will but Thine, I will have no self but Thee.

255 The Church Within Us

Kent Schneider   Kent Schneider

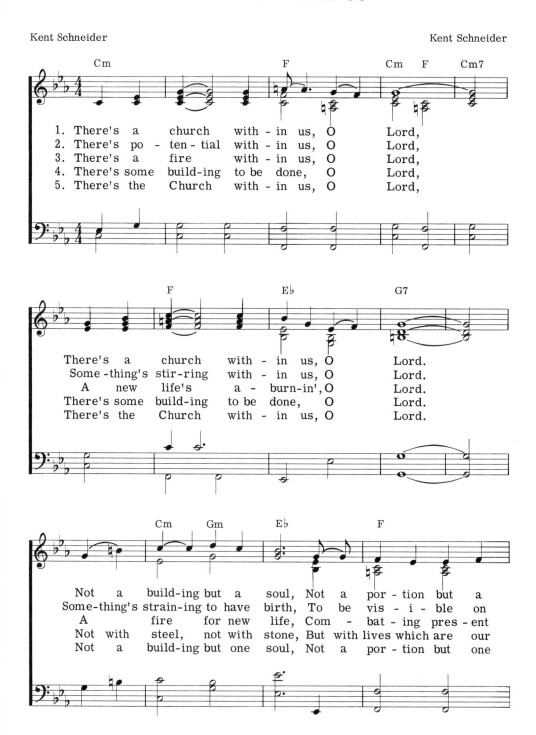

1. There's a church with-in us, O Lord,
2. There's po-ten-tial with-in us, O Lord,
3. There's a fire with-in us, O Lord,
4. There's some build-ing to be done, O Lord,
5. There's the Church with-in us, O Lord,

There's a church with-in us, O Lord.
Some-thing's stir-ring with-in us, O Lord.
A new life's a-burn-in', O Lord.
There's some build-ing to be done, O Lord.
There's the Church with-in us, O Lord.

Not a build-ing but a soul, Not a por-tion but a
Some-thing's strain-ing to have birth, To be vis-i-ble on
A fire for new life, Com-bat-ing pres-ent
Not with steel, not with stone, But with lives which are our
Not a build-ing but one soul, Not a por-tion but one

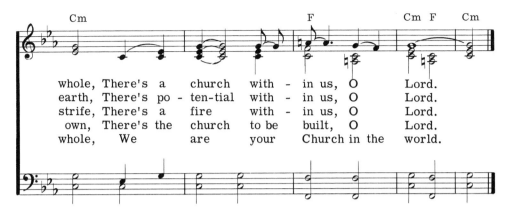

whole, There's a church with - in us, O Lord.
earth, There's po - ten-tial with - in us, O Lord.
strife, There's a fire with - in us, O Lord.
own, There's the church to be built, O Lord.
whole, We are your Church in the world.

I Am Filled

256

Refrain adapted from
Eliza E. Hewitt

John R. Sweney

I am filled, I am filled to o - ver - flow - ing, to o - ver-

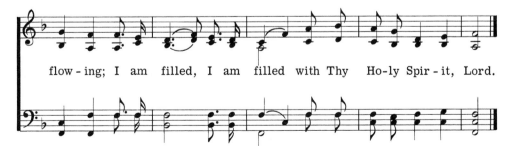

flow - ing; I am filled, I am filled with Thy Ho-ly Spir - it, Lord.

257   Rock of Ages, Truth Divine

Anonymous

TOPLADY
Thomas Hastings

1. Rock of a - ges, Truth di - vine, Strong foun -
2. On the rock of Truth I stand, Des - ti -
3. For the ask - ing I at - tain Ev - ery

da - tion, ev - er mine; Safe, se - cure, I here re -
ny at my com - mand; Filled with peace and power of
height in Truth's do - main, Ev - ery wish with - in my

main, In the peace He doth or - dain; Liv - ing
God, Bound - less good, e - ter - nal love; Safe with
heart; For no bless - ing can de - part. All of

ev - er in the light, Pure and per - fect in God's sight.
Truth, so firm and strong, Prais-ing in tri - um-phant song.
good is ev - er mine, On the rock of Truth di - vine.

More Love to Thee

258

MORE LOVE TO THEE
William H. Doane

Elizabeth P. Prentiss, adapted

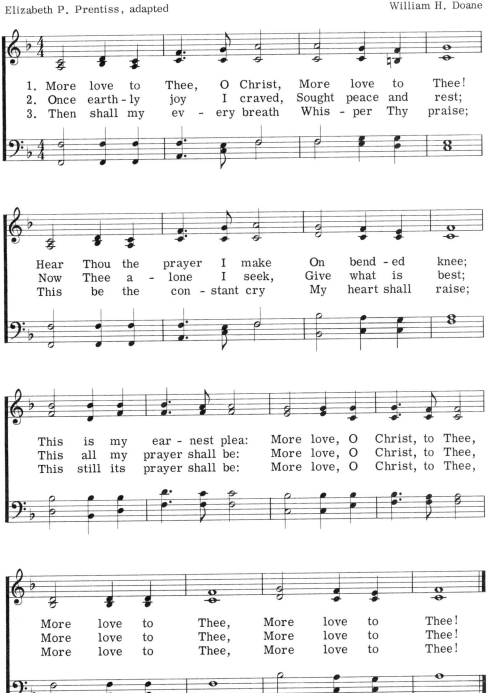

1. More love to Thee, O Christ, More love to Thee!
2. Once earth-ly joy I craved, Sought peace and rest;
3. Then shall my ev - ery breath Whis - per Thy praise;

Hear Thou the prayer I make On bend - ed knee;
Now Thee a - lone I seek, Give what is best;
This be the con - stant cry My heart shall raise;

This is my ear - nest plea: More love, O Christ, to Thee,
This all my prayer shall be: More love, O Christ, to Thee,
This still its prayer shall be: More love, O Christ, to Thee,

More love to Thee, More love to Thee!
More love to Thee, More love to Thee!
More love to Thee, More love to Thee!

259   O Come, Little Children

Translated from Christoph von Schmid

IHR KINDERLEIN KOMMET
Johann A. P. Schulz

1. O come, lit-tle chil-dren, O come, one and all! O come to the cra-dle in Beth-le-hem's stall, And see what the Fa-ther, from high heaven a-bove, Has sent us to-night as a proof of His love.

2. O see where He's ly-ing, the heav-en-ly Boy! Here Jo-seph and Mar-y be-hold Him with joy; The shep-herds have come, and are kneel-ing in prayer, While songs of the an-gels float o-ver Him there.

O Come, O Come, Emmanuel

Latin, c. 9th Century
Translation by John M. Neale and
Henry S. Coffin

VENI EMMANUEL
Adapted from Plainsong
by Thomas Helmore

Unison

1. O come, O come, Em - man - u - el, And ran-som cap - tive
2. O come, thou Wis - dom from on high, And or - der all things
3. O come, De - sire of na - tions, bind All peo-ples in one

Is - ra - el, That mourns in lone - ly ex - ile here, Un -
far and nigh; To us the path of knowl-edge show, And
heart and mind; Bid en - vy, strife, and quar -rels cease; Fill

Refrain

til the Son of God ap - pear.
cause us in her ways to go. Re - joice! Re - joice! Em-
the whole world with heav - en's peace.

man - u - el Shall come to thee, O Is - ra - el!

Of the Father's Love Begotten

DIVINUM MYSTERIUM
13th Century Plainsong, Mode V
From *The Hymnal 1940*
Arr. by C. Winfred Douglas

Aurelius Clemens Prudentius
Translation by John M. Neale and
Henry W. Baker

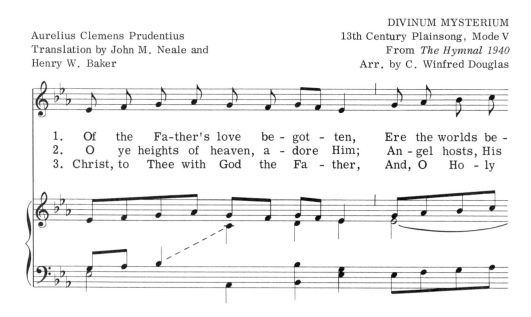

1. Of the Fa-ther's love be-got-ten, Ere the worlds be-
2. O ye heights of heaven, a-dore Him; An-gel hosts, His
3. Christ, to Thee with God the Fa-ther, And, O Ho-ly

gan to be, He is Al-pha and O-me-ga,
prais-es sing; Powers, do-min-ions, bow be-fore Him,
Ghost, to Thee, Hymn and chant and high thanks-giv-ing,

He the source, the end - ing He; Of the things that are, that
And ex - tol our God and King; Let no tongue on earth be
And un - wea - ried prais - es be: Hon-or, glo - ry, and do -

have   been,   And that fu - ture years shall see,
si -   lent,   Ev - ery voice in con - cert ring,
min -   ion,   And e - ter - nal vic - to - ry,

Ev - er - more and ev - er - more.
Ev - er - more and ev - er - more.
Ev - er - more and ev - er - more.   A - men.

262   Lo, How a Rose E'er Blooming

German, 15th century
Translation by Theodore Baker

ES IST EIN' ROS'
German Melody
Arr. by Michael Praetorius

1. Lo, how a Rose e'er bloom - ing From ten- der stem
2. I - sa-iah 'twas fore-told it, The Rose I have

hath sprung! Of Jes-se's lin-eage com - ing As
in mind, With Mar - y we be-hold it, The

men of old have sung. It came, a
Vir - gin Moth - er kind. To show God's

flower - et bright, A - mid the cold of win -
love a - right, She bore to men a Sav -

ter, When half spent was the night.
ior, When half spent was the night.

There's a Song in the Air

CHRISTMAS SONG

Josiah G. Holland

Karl P. Harrington

1. There's a song in the air! There's a star in the sky!
2. There's a tu-mult of joy O'er the won-der-ful birth,
3. In the light of that star Lie the a-ges im-pearled;
4. We re-joice in the light, And we ech-o the song

There's a moth-er's deep prayer And a ba-by's low cry!
For the vir-gin's sweet boy Is the Lord of the earth.
And that song from a-far Has swept o-ver the world.
That comes down through the night From the heav-en-ly throng.

And the star rains its fire while the beau-ti-ful sing,
Ay! the star rains its fire while the beau-ti-ful sing,
Ev-ery hearth is a-flame, and the beau-ti-ful sing
Ay! we shout to the love-ly e-van-gel they bring,

For the man-ger of Beth-le-hem cra-dles a King!
For the man-ger of Beth-le-hem cra-dles a King!
In the homes of the na-tions that Je-sus is King!
And we greet in His cra-dle our Sav-ior and King!

264 All My Heart This Night Rejoices

Paul Gerhardt
Translation by Catherine Winkworth

WARUM SOLLT ICH
Johann G. Ebeling

1. All my heart this night re - joic - es As I hear,
2. Hark! a voice from yon - der man - ger, Soft and sweet,
3. Come, then, let us has - ten yon - der! Here let all,

Far and near, Sweet - est an - gel voic - es.
Doth en - treat: "Flee from woe and dan - ger!
Great and small, Kneel in awe and won - der!

"Christ is born," their choirs are sing - ing,
Breth - ren, come! from all doth grieve you,
Love Him who with love is yearn - ing!

Till the air Ev - ery - where Now with joy is ring - ing.
You are freed; All you need I will sure - ly give you."
Hail the star That from far Bright with hope is burn - ing!

Sweet Bells of Heaven

Mary E. Butters

Clara H. Scott

1. Sweet bells of heaven, how glad ye ring Of heaven-ly Love, our new-born King! Deep-toned and pure and true as steel, Ye touch on chords that bind and heal; Ye touch on chords that bind and heal.

2. Sweet bells of heaven, ye are a song, A song of praise, the whole day long! When lis-tening in the si-lence sweet I catch the foot-falls of Christ's feet; I catch the foot-falls of Christ's feet.

3. I hear the mys-tic puls-es fall Of one Great Heart that beats for all; From low-ly peas-ant, prince, to King, Sweet bells of heaven, for-ev-er ring! Sweet bells of heaven, for-ev-er ring!

266 My Soul Doth Magnify the Lord

Francis J. Gable

CHRISTMAS PRAISE
Carl Frangkiser

1. My soul doth mag-ni-fy the Lord, My spir-it is re-joic-ing; Good will and peace to all man-kind My hap-py heart is voic-ing.

2. The new-born Babe at Beth-le-hem Re-news the old, old sto-ry; His Spir-it lives a-gain in me And fills my life with glo-ry.

3. My soul doth mag-ni-fy the Lord For price-less gift of liv-ing, And for the Christ that teach-es me To know the joy of giv-ing.

Refrain Unison

Glo-ry to God, glo-ry to God,

267   The First Noel

Traditional English Carol

THE FIRST NOEL
Traditional English Tune

1. The first No - el, the an - gel did
2. They look - ed up and saw a
3. This star drew nigh to the north -
4. Then en - tered in those wise men

say, Was to cer - tain poor shep-herds in fields as they
star Shin -ing in the east, be - yond them
west, O'er Beth - le - hem it took its
three, Full rev - erent - ly up - on the

lay; In fields where they lay keep - ing their
far; And to the earth it gave great
rest, And there it did both stop and
knee, And of - fered there, in His pres -

sheep, On a cold win-ter's night that was so deep.
light, And so it con - tin -ued both day and night.
stay, Right o - ver the place where Je - sus lay.
ence, Their gold and myrrh and frank - in - cense.

No - el,   No - el,   No - el,   No -

el,   Born is the King of Is - ra - el.

268   What Child Is This

GREENSLEEVES
Traditional English Melody
Harmonized by John Stainer

William C. Dix

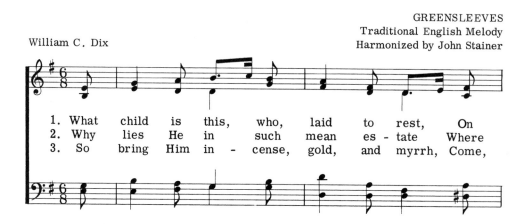

1. What child is this, who, laid to rest, On
2. Why lies He in such mean es - tate Where
3. So bring Him in - cense, gold, and myrrh, Come,

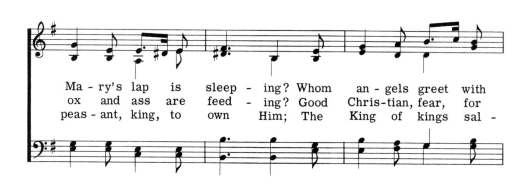

Ma - ry's lap is sleep - ing? Whom an - gels greet with
ox and ass are feed - ing? Good Chris-tian, fear, for
peas - ant, king, to own Him; The King of kings sal -

an - thems sweet, While shep - herds watch are keep - ing?
sin - ners here The si - lent Word is plead - ing.
va - tion brings, Let lov - ing hearts en - throne Him.

This, this is Christ the King, Whom

shep - herds guard and an - gels sing; Haste, haste to

bring Him laud, The Babe, the Son of Ma - ry.

269   Go, Tell It on the Mountain

American Folk Hymn
Words adapted by John W. Work II

GO TELL IT ON THE MOUNTAIN
American Folk Hymn
Harmonization by John W. Work III

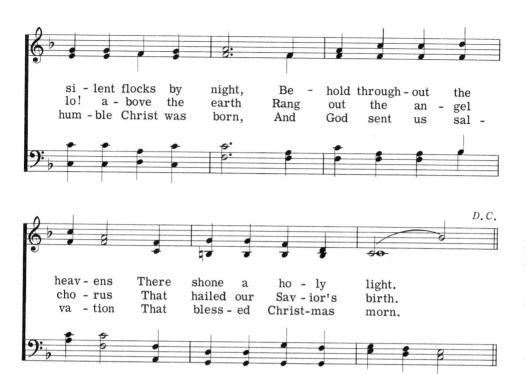

si - lent flocks by night, Be - hold through - out the
lo! a - bove the earth Rang out the an - gel
hum - ble Christ was born, And God sent us sal -

D.C.

heav - ens There shone a ho - ly light.
cho - rus That hailed our Sav - ior's birth.
va - tion That bless - ed Christ-mas morn.

270 Silent Night, Holy Night

Joseph Mohr
Translation by John F. Young
Stanza 4: *Unity Song Selections*

STILLE NACHT
Franz Gruber

1. Si - lent night, ho - ly night, All is calm,
2. Si - lent night, ho - ly night, Shep - herds quake
3. Si - lent night, ho - ly night, Son of God,
4. Ho - ly light, per - fect light, Christ of God,

all is bright Round yon vir - gin moth - er and child.
at the sight, Glo - ries stream from heav - en a - far,
love's pure light Ra - diant beams from Thy ho - ly face,
oh, how bright Doth Thy Spir - it shine al - way!

Ho - ly in - fant so ten - der and mild, Sleep in heav - en - ly
Heaven - ly hosts sing al - le - lu - ia; Christ the Sav - ior is
With the dawn of re - deem - ing grace, Je - sus, Lord at Thy
Heal - ing, bless - ing man each day With Thy heav - en - ly

peace, Sleep in heav - en - ly peace.
born! Christ the Sav - ior is born!
birth, Je - sus, Lord, at Thy birth.
love, With Thy heav - en - ly love.

Away in a Manger

AWAY IN A MANGER
James R. Murray

Anonymous

1. A - way in a man - ger, no crib for a bed,
2. The cat - tle are low - ing, the ba - by a - wakes,

The lit - tle Lord Je - sus laid down His sweet head.
But lit - tle Lord Je - sus, no cry - ing He makes.

The stars in the sky looked down where He lay,
I love Thee, Lord Je - sus, look down from the sky,

The lit - tle Lord Je - sus, a - sleep on the hay.
And stay by my cra - dle to watch lul - la - by.

272   It Came upon the Midnight Clear

Edmund H. Sears

CAROL
Richard S. Willis

1. It came up-on the mid - night clear, That
2. Still through the clo - ven skies they come With
3. For lo! the days are has - tening on, By

glo - rious song of old, From
peace - ful wings un - furled, And
proph - et bards fore - told, When

an - gels bend - ing near the earth, To
still their heaven - ly mu - sic floats O'er
with the ev - er - cir - cling years Comes

touch their harps of gold: "Peace
all the wea - ry world; A -
round the age of gold; When

273 O Little Town of Bethlehem

Phillips Brooks

ST. LOUIS
Lewis H. Redner

1. O lit - tle town of Beth - le - hem, How still we see thee lie; A - bove thy deep and dream - less sleep The si - lent stars go by; Yet in thy dark streets shin - eth The

2. For Christ is born of Ma - ry; And gath - ered all a - bove, While mor - tals sleep, the an - gels keep Their watch of won - dering love. O morn - ing stars, to - geth - er Pro -

3. How si - lent - ly, how si - lent - ly The won - drous gift is given! So God im - parts to hu - man hearts The bless - ings of His heaven. No ear may hear His com - ing, But

4. O ho - ly Child of Beth - le - hem, De - scend on us, we pray; Cast out our sin, and en - ter in, Be born in us to - day. We hear the Christ - mas an - gels The

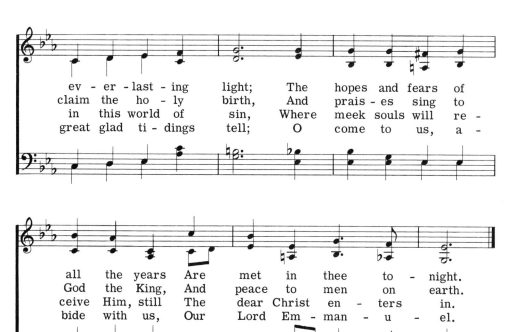

ev - er - last - ing light; The hopes and fears of
claim the ho - ly birth, And prais - es sing to
in this world of sin, Where meek souls will re -
great glad ti - dings tell; O come to us, a -

all the years Are met in thee to - night.
God the King, And peace to men on earth.
ceive Him, still The dear Christ en - ters in.
bide with us, Our Lord Em - man - u - el.

274   Hark! The Herald Angels Sing

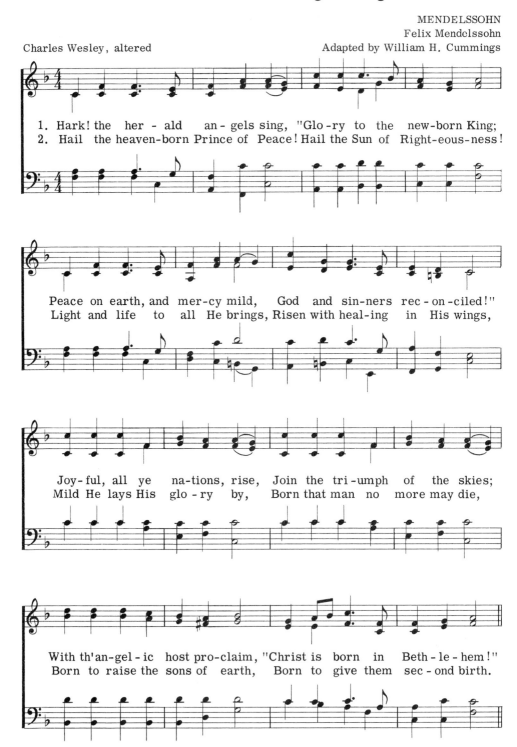

MENDELSSOHN
Felix Mendelssohn
Charles Wesley, altered   Adapted by William H. Cummings

1. Hark! the her - ald an - gels sing, "Glo -ry to the new-born King;
2. Hail the heaven-born Prince of Peace! Hail the Sun of Right-eous-ness!

Peace on earth, and mer-cy mild, God and sin-ners rec - on -ciled!"
Light and life to all He brings, Risen with heal-ing in His wings,

Joy-ful, all ye na-tions, rise, Join the tri-umph of the skies;
Mild He lays His glo-ry by, Born that man no more may die,

With th'an-gel-ic host pro-claim, "Christ is born in Beth-le-hem!"
Born to raise the sons of earth, Born to give them sec-ond birth.

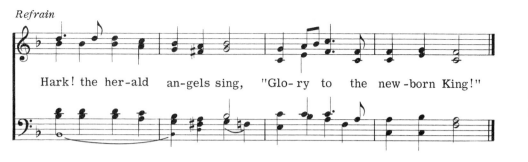

Refrain

Hark! the her-ald an-gels sing, "Glo-ry to the new-born King!"

Make Me a Blessing, Lord 275

Make me a blessing, Lord! Help me
To help those needing help, to be
A blessing to my fellow men.
Instruct me when to speak and when
To hold my speech, when to be bold
In giving and when to withhold;
And if I have not strength enough,
Then give me strength. Lord, make me tough
With my own self but tender toward
All others. Let there be outpoured
On me the gentleness to bless
All who have need of gentleness.
Give me a word, a touch to fill
The lonely life, faith for the ill,
And courage to keep hearts up though
My own is feeling just as low.
When men have bitter things to meet
And quail and would accept defeat,
Then let me lift their eyes to see
The vision of Thy victory.
Help me to help; help me to give
The wisdom and the will to live!

—James Dillet Freeman

276 Behold the Star

Vivian Yeiser Laramore

CHRISTMAS GREETING
Carl Frangkiser

1. Be - hold the star, the won - drous star That
2. Up - on this day His love su - preme Re -

leads to Christ in you! The wise have fol - lowed
lights the in - ner flame, And we who walked as

from a - far And found the prom - ise true. Oh,
in a dream A - wake to know His name; For

let the bells in rap - ture ring And
He is here whom we a - dore, Oh,

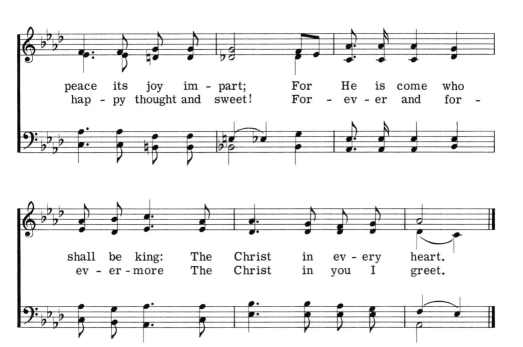

peace its joy im - part; For He is come who
hap - py thought and sweet! For - ev - er and for -

shall be king: The Christ in ev - ery heart.
ev - er - more The Christ in you I greet.

277   Angels, from the Realms of Glory

James Montgomery

REGENT SQUARE
Henry T. Smart

1. An - gels, from the realms of glo - ry,
2. Shep - herds, in the fields a - bid - ing,
3. Sag - es, leave your con - tem - pla - tions,

Wing your flight o'er all the earth; Ye who sang cre -
Watch-ing o'er your flocks by night, God with man is
Bright-er vi - sions beam a - far; Seek the great De -

a - tion's sto - ry, Now pro-claim Mes - si -ah's birth:
now re - sid - ing, Yon - der shines the in - fant light:
sire of na - tions, Ye have seen His na - tal star:

Refrain

Come and wor - ship, come and wor - ship,

Wor - ship Christ, the new - born King.

I Heard the Bells 278

WALTHAM
John B. Calkin

Henry W. Longfellow

1. I heard the bells on Christ - mas Day Their
2. I thought how, as the day had come, The
3. Till ring - ing, sing - ing on its way, The

old fa - mil - iar car - ols play, And wild and sweet The
bel-fries of all Chris - ten-dom Had rolled a - long Th'un -
world re - volved from night to day— A voice, a chime, A

words re - peat, Of "Peace on earth, good will to men!"
brok - en song, Of "Peace on earth, good will to men!"
chant sub - lime, Of "Peace on earth, good will to men!"

279   Angels We Have Heard on High

GLORIA
Traditional French Carol

Traditional French Carol

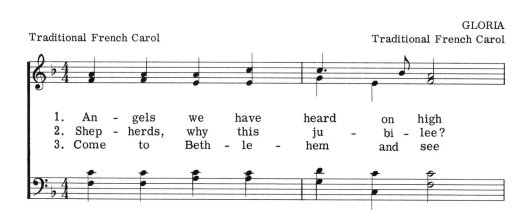

1. An - gels we have heard on high
2. Shep - herds, why this ju - bi - lee?
3. Come to Beth - le - hem and see

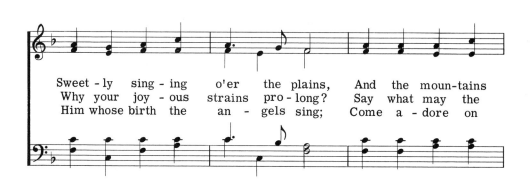

Sweet - ly sing - ing o'er the plains, And the moun - tains
Why your joy - ous strains pro - long? Say what may the
Him whose birth the an - gels sing; Come a - dore on

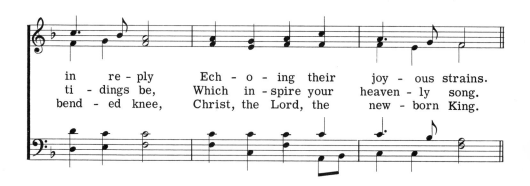

in re - ply Ech - o - ing their joy - ous strains.
ti - dings be, Which in - spire your heaven - ly song.
bend - ed knee, Christ, the Lord, the new - born King.

280 Joy to the World

ANTIOCH
Arr. from George Frederick Handel
by Lowell Mason

Isaac Watts

1. Joy to the world! the Lord is come: Let
2. Joy to the world! the Sav - ior reigns: Let
3. He rules the world with truth and grace, And

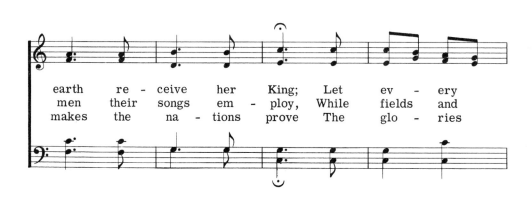

earth re - ceive her King; Let ev - ery
men their songs em - ploy, While fields and
makes the na - tions prove The glo - ries

heart pre - pare Him room, And
floods, rocks, hills, and plains Re -
of His right - eous - ness, And

heaven and na - ture sing, And heaven and na - ture
peat the sound -ing joy, Re - peat the sound -ing
won - ders of His love, And won - ders of His

And heaven and na - ture sing, And
Re - peat the sound-ing joy, Re -
And won - ders of His love, And

sing, And heaven, and heaven and na - ture sing.
joy, Re - peat, re - peat the sound -ing joy.
love, And won - ders, won - ders of His love.

heaven and na -ture sing,
peat the sound-ing joy,
won-ders of His love,

281   We Three Kings

John H. Hopkins, Jr.

KINGS OF ORIENT
John H. Hopkins, Jr.

1. We three kings of O - ri - ent are; Bear - ing
5. Glo - rious now be - hold Him a - rise, King and

gifts we tra - verse a - far, Field and foun - tain,
God and Sac - ri - fice; Al - le - lu - ia,

moor and moun - tain, Fol - low - ing yon - der star.
al - le - lu - ia! Sounds through the earth and skies.

Refrain

O star of won - der, star of night, Star with

roy - al beau - ty bright, West-ward lead - ing, still pro - ceed - ing, Guide us to thy per - fect light.

2. Born a King on Bethlehem's plain,
   Gold I bring to crown Him again,
   King forever, ceasing never
   Over us all to reign. *(Refrain)*

3. Frankincense to offer have I,
   Incense owns a Deity nigh;
   Prayer and praising, all men raising,
   Worship Him, God on high. *(Refrain)*

4. Myrrh is mine: its bitter perfume
   Breathes a life of gathering gloom:
   Sorrowing, sighing, bleeding, dying,
   Sealed in the stone-cold tomb. *(Refrain)*

282 While by My Sheep

JUNGST
German Melody
Arranged by Hugo Jungst

German Carol

1. While by my sheep I watched at night,
2. There shall be born, so he did say,
3. There shall the Child lie in a stall,
4. This gift of God I'll cher - ish well,

Glad tid - ings brought an an - gel bright.
In Beth - le - hem a Child to - day;
This Child who shall re - deem us all.
That ev - er joy my heart shall fill.

Refrain

f   *pp echo*   *f*

How great my joy! Great my joy! Joy, joy, joy!

pp echo   *f*

Joy, joy, joy! Praise we the Lord in heaven on

high! Praise we the Lord in heaven on high!

Love Came Down at Christmas 283

Christina G. Rossetti

GARTON
Trad. Irish Melody

1. Love came down at Christ-mas, Love all love - ly, Love di - vine;
2. Love shall be our to - ken, Love be yours and love be mine,

Love was born at Christ - mas, Star and an - gels gave the sign.
Love to God and all men, Love for plea and gift and sign.

284   God Rest You Merry, Gentlemen

GOD REST YOU MERRY
18th Century English Melody
Arranged by John Stainer

18th Century English Carol

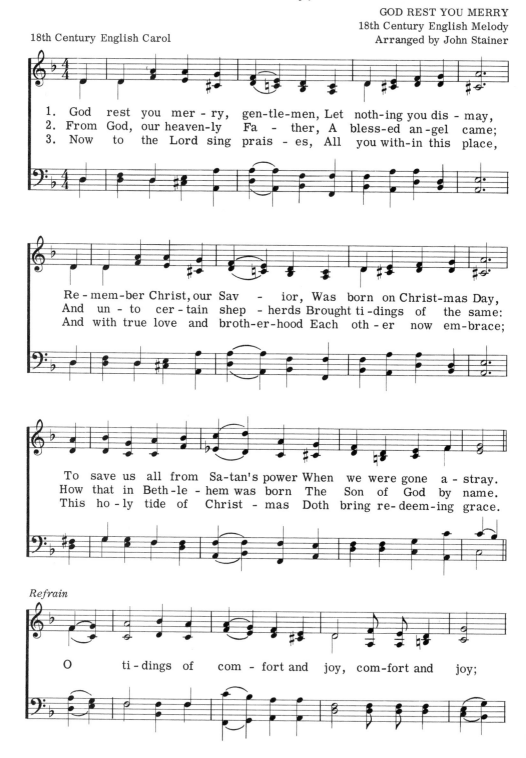

1. God rest you mer-ry, gen-tle-men, Let noth-ing you dis-may,
2. From God, our heaven-ly Fa - ther, A bless-ed an-gel came;
3. Now to the Lord sing prais - es, All you with-in this place,

Re-mem-ber Christ, our Sav - ior, Was born on Christ-mas Day,
And un - to cer-tain shep - herds Brought ti-dings of the same:
And with true love and broth-er-hood Each oth - er now em-brace;

To save us all from Sa-tan's power When we were gone a-stray.
How that in Beth-le-hem was born The Son of God by name.
This ho-ly tide of Christ - mas Doth bring re-deem-ing grace.

Refrain

O ti-dings of com - fort and joy, com-fort and joy;

O ti - dings of com - fort and joy!

Christmas Bells

285

LOVELY EVENING
Traditional English Round

Unity in Song

1. It's a time of Christ-mas giv - ing, Christ-mas
2. It's a time of Christ-mas sing - ing, Christ-mas
3. Fill the air with Christ-mas spir - it, Christ-mas
4. Let's en - joy the Christ-mas spir - it, Christ-mas

giv - ing, When the bells are sweet-ly ring - ing,
sing - ing; Hear the bells so sweet-ly ring - ing,
spir - it; Let the bells keep sweet-ly ring - ing,
spir - it; While the bells keep sweet-ly ring - ing,

sweet-ly ring - ing, Ding, dong, ding, dong.
sweet-ly ring - ing, Ding, dong, ding, dong.
sweet-ly ring - ing, Ding, dong, ding, dong.
sweet-ly ring - ing, Ding, dong, ding, dong.

286   O Come, All Ye Faithful

Attributed to John F. Wade
Based on tr. by Frederick Oakeley

ADESTE FIDELES
J. F. Wade's *Cantus Diversi*

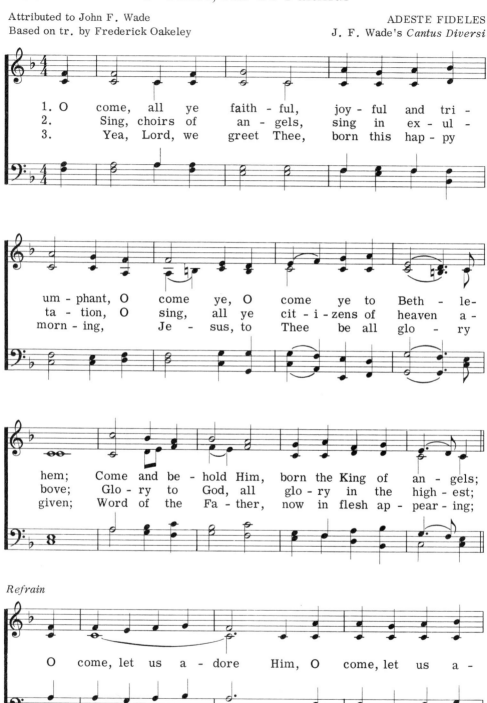

1. O come, all ye faith - ful, joy - ful and tri - um - phant, O come ye, O come ye to Beth - le - hem; Come and be - hold Him, born the King of an - gels;

2. Sing, choirs of an - gels, sing in ex - ul - ta - tion, O sing, all ye cit - i - zens of heaven a - bove; Glo - ry to God, all glo - ry in the high - est;

3. Yea, Lord, we greet Thee, born this hap - py morn - ing, Je - sus, to Thee be all glo - ry given; Word of the Fa - ther, now in flesh ap - pear - ing;

Refrain

O come, let us a - dore Him, O come, let us a -

dore Him, O come, let us a - dore Him, Christ, the Lord!

Adeste Fideles 287

Attributed to John F. Wade

ADESTE FIDELES
J. F. Wade's *Cantus Diversi*

1. Adeste fideles,
   Laeti triumphantes,
   Venite, venite in Bethlehem.
   Natum videte
   Regem angelorum.
   Venite, adoremus,
   Venite, adoremus,
   Venite, adoremus Dominum.

2. Ergo qui natus
   Die hodierna,
   Jesu, tibi sit gloria.
   Patris aeterni
   Verbum caro factum.
   Venite, adoremus,
   Venite, adoremus,
   Venite, adoremus Dominum.

288 While Shepherds Watched Their Flocks

CHRISTMAS
Nahum Tate
Arranged from George Frederick Handel

1. While shep-herds watched their flocks by night, All
2. All glo - ry be to God on high, And

seat - ed on the ground, The an - gel of the
to the earth be peace: Good will hence-forth from

Lord came down, And glo - ry shone a -
heaven to men Be - gin and nev - er

round, And glo - ry shone a - round.
cease! Be - gin and nev - er cease!

Good Christian Men, Rejoice

IN DULCI JUBILO
14th Century German Melody
Harmonized by V. Earle Copes

Latin, 14th Century
Paraphrase by John M. Neale

Unison

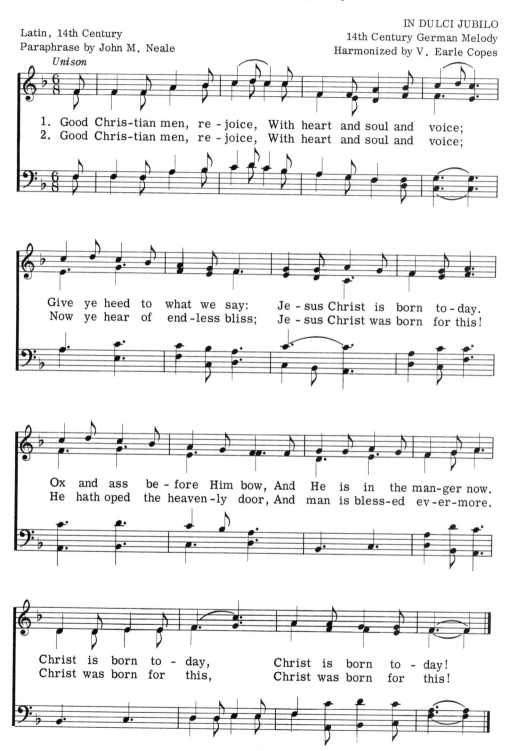

1. Good Chris-tian men, re-joice, With heart and soul and voice;
2. Good Chris-tian men, re-joice, With heart and soul and voice;

Give ye heed to what we say: Je-sus Christ is born to-day.
Now ye hear of end-less bliss; Je-sus Christ was born for this!

Ox and ass be-fore Him bow, And He is in the man-ger now.
He hath oped the heaven-ly door, And man is bless-ed ev-er-more.

Christ is born to-day, Christ is born to-day!
Christ was born for this, Christ was born for this!

290 The Wondrous Story

Francis J. Gable

Carl Frangkiser

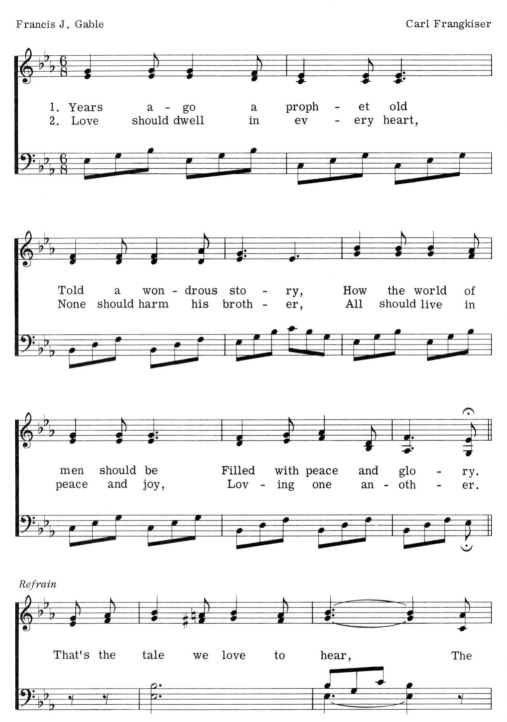

1. Years a-go a proph-et old
2. Love should dwell in ev-ery heart,

Told a won-drous sto-ry, How the world of
None should harm his broth-er, All should live in

men should be Filled with peace and glo-ry.
peace and joy, Lov-ing one an-oth-er.

Refrain

That's the tale we love to hear, The

tale   of Christ-mas   morn,   When,   to bring   us

joy   and cheer,   Christ our King was   born.

291 Merry Christmas

Bill Provost

Bill Provost

Brightly (not too fast)

1. Mer - ry Christ - mas! Christ is born with - in us;
2. Hal - le - lu - jah! Let the Christ with - in us

It's a ver - y ex - tra - or - di - nar - y day.
Ra - di - ate, so we can cel - e -

(to verse 2.)

brate this day. Make a joy - ful sound; Let

sleigh bells jin - gle; Joy is al - ways found when

292 All Glory, Laud, and Honor

Theodulph of Orleans
Translation, John M. Neale

ST. THEODULPH
Melchior Teschner

1. All glo-ry, laud, and hon-or To Thee, Re-deem-er,
2. The com-pa-ny of an-gels Are prais-ing Thee on
3. Thou didst ac-cept their prais-es; Ac-cept the prayers we

King, To whom the lips of chil - dren Made
high, And mor-tal men and all things Cre-
bring, Who in all good de - light - est, Thou

sweet ho-san-nas ring! Thou art the King of
at-ed make re - ply. The peo-ple of the
good and gra-cious King. All glo-ry, laud, and

Is - rael, Thou Da-vid's roy-al Son, Who
He - brews With palms be-fore Thee went; Our
hon - or To Thee, Re-deem-er, King, To

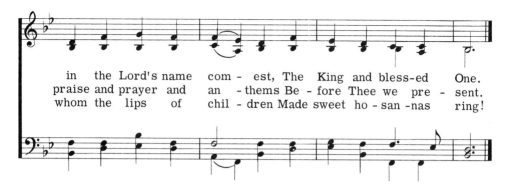

in the Lord's name com - est, The King and bless-ed One.
praise and prayer and an - thems Be - fore Thee we pre - sent.
whom the lips of chil - dren Made sweet ho - san -nas ring!

The Heavens Thy Praise Are Telling 293

Anonymous

ST. THEODULPH
Melchior Teachner

1. The heavens Thy praise are telling,
   The earth declares Thy might,
But naught save Thine indwelling
   Can show Thee, Lord, aright.
Where'er our eyes are turning,
   Thy footprints we can see,
The light within us burning
   Alone revealeth Thee.

2. We know no life divided,
   O Lord of life, from Thee;
In Thee is life provided
   For all humanity.
We know no death, O Spirit,
   Because we live in Thee,
And all our souls inherit
   Thine immortality.

294 Hosanna, Loud Hosanna

ELLACOMBE
Jeannette Threlfall
Gesangbuch, Wirtemberg, 1784

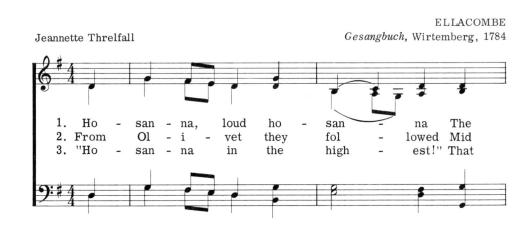

1. Ho - san - na, loud ho - san - na The
2. From Ol - i - vet they fol - lowed Mid
3. "Ho - san - na in the high - est!" That

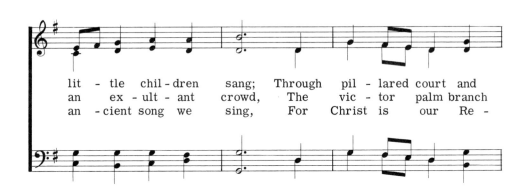

lit - tle chil - dren sang; Through pil - lared court and
an ex - ult - ant crowd, The vic - tor palm branch
an - cient song we sing, For Christ is our Re -

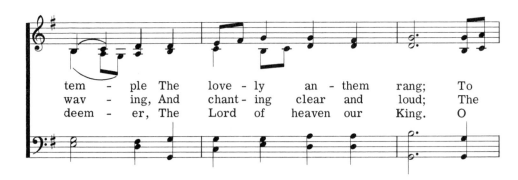

tem - ple The love - ly an - them rang; To
wav - ing, And chant - ing clear and loud; The
deem - er, The Lord of heaven our King. O

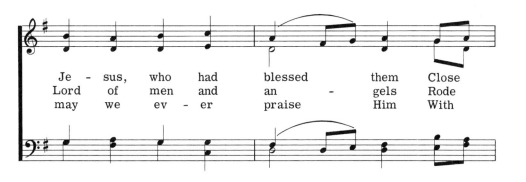

Je - sus, who had blessed them Close
Lord of men and an - gels Rode
may we ev - er praise Him With

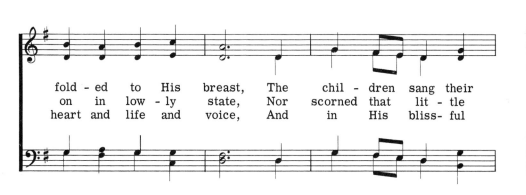

fold - ed to His breast, The chil - dren sang their
on in low - ly state, Nor scorned that lit - tle
heart and life and voice, And in His bliss- ful

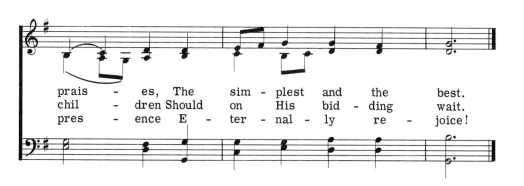

prais - es, The sim - plest and the best.
chil - dren Should on His bid - ding wait.
pres - ence E - ter - nal - ly re - joice!

295 The Day of Resurrection

John of Damascus
Translation, John M. Neale, alt.

LANCASHIRE
Henry Smart

1. The day of res-ur-rec-tion! Earth, tell it out a-
2. Now let the heavens be joy-ful! Let earth her song be-

broad; The Pass-o-ver of glad-ness, The
gin! Let all the world keep tri-umph, And

Pass-o-ver of God. From death to life e-
all that is there-in. Let all things seen and

ter-nal, From earth un-to the sky, Our
un-seen Their notes in glad-ness blend, For

Christ hath brought us o-ver With hymns of vic-to-ry.
Christ the Lord is ris-en, Our joy that hath no end.

Eternal Life Is Here

SANTA LUCIA
Arranged from Teodoro Cottrau

Unity Song Selections

1. E - ter - nal life is here! Sus - tain - ing pow - er!
2. E - ter - nal life is here! That life is won - drous love!
3. E - ter - nal life is here! I've sown this pre - cious seed,

A ra - diant light to me through ev - ery hour.
My life is cen-tered in the life of God.
And now I feel its power in word and deed.

E - ter-nal life is here! O what a won-drous thought!
E - ter-nal life is here! I rest in joy and peace;
E - ter-nal life is here! This life is full and free!

A might-y truth to me these words have taught.
And as I live in God, all joys in - crease.
The dawn - ing light of Truth I clear - ly see.

297   Now Let the Vault of Heaven Resound

LASST UNS ERFREUEN
Melody from *Geistliche Kirchengesänge,* 1623
Paul Zeller Strodach, 1876-1947
Arr. by Ralph Vaughan Williams, 1872-1958

1. Now let the vault of heaven re - sound In praise of Love that doth a - bound, "Christ hath tri - umphed, Al - le - lu - ia!" Sing,
2. E - ter - nal is the gift He brings, Where - fore our heart with rap - ture sings, "Christ hath tri - umphed, Je - sus liv - eth!" Now
3. O fill us, Lord, with daunt - less love; Set heart and will on things a - bove That we con - quer through Thy tri - umph. Grant
4. A - dor - ing prais - es now we bring And with the heaven - ly bless - ed sing, "Christ hath tri - umphed, Al - le - lu - ia!" Be

298
He Is Risen

Mrs. C. F. Alexander

Charles M. Fillmore

1. He is ris - en, He is ris - en, Tell it
2. He is ris - en, He is ris - en, He hath
3. Bless - ed Lord, let all a - dore Thee, Saints on

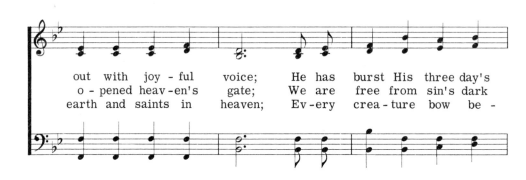

out with joy - ful voice; He has burst His three day's
o - pened heav -en's gate; We are free from sin's dark
earth and saints in heaven; Ev -ery crea -ture bow be -

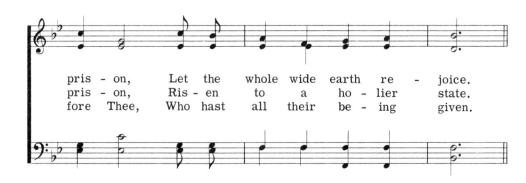

pris - on, Let the whole wide earth re - joice.
pris - on, Ris - en to a ho - lier state.
fore Thee, Who hast all their be - ing given.

Christ is ris - en, Hal - le - lu - jah! Christ is

ris - en, Hal - le - lu - jah! Christ is ris - en, Hal - le -

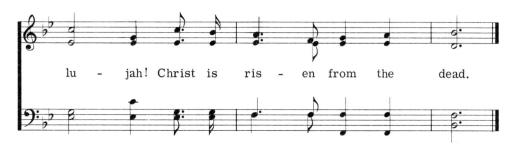

lu - jah! Christ is ris - en from the dead.

299 Alleluia

Alleluias from VICTORY
Adapted by William H. Monk
from Giovanni P. da Palestrina

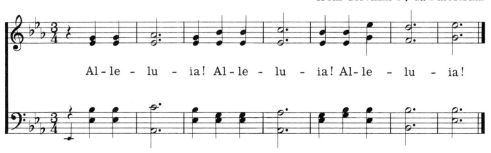

Al - le - lu - ia! Al - le - lu - ia! Al - le - lu - ia!

300 Christ the Lord Is Risen Today

Charles Wesley
Stanzas 2 and 3, Anonymous

EASTER HYMN
Lyra Davidica

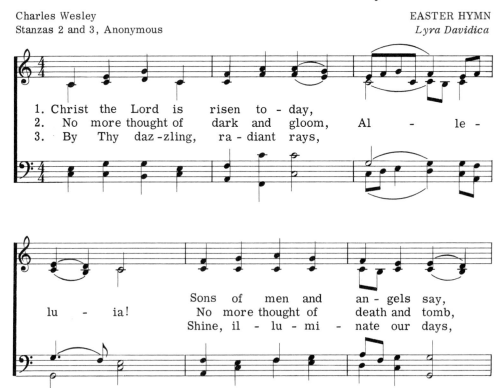

1. Christ the Lord is risen to - day,
2. No more thought of dark and gloom, Al - le -
3. By Thy daz-zling, ra - diant rays,

lu - ia!
Sons of men and an - gels say,
No more thought of death and tomb,
Shine, il - lu - mi - nate our days,

301 Lord of the Dance

Sydney Carter

Traditional
Arr. and adapted by Sydney Carter

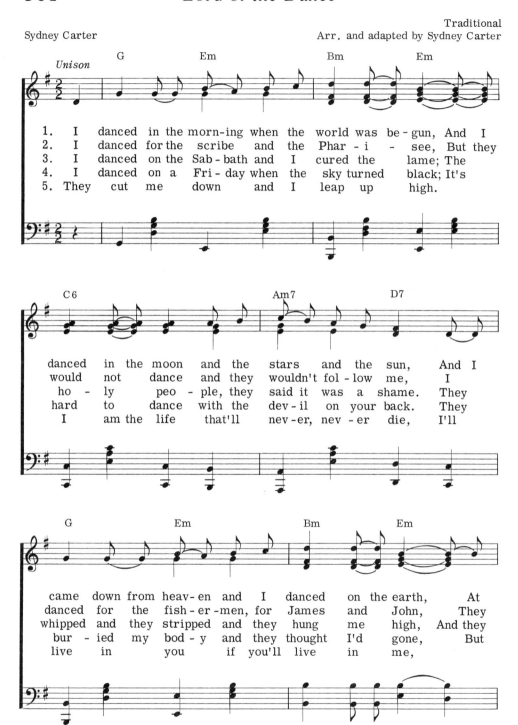

1. I danced in the morn-ing when the world was be-gun, And I danced in the moon and the stars and the sun, And I came down from heav-en and I danced on the earth, At
2. I danced for the scribe and the Phar-i-see, But they would not dance and they wouldn't fol-low me, I danced for the fish-er-men, for James and John, They
3. I danced on the Sab-bath and I cured the lame; The ho-ly peo-ple, they said it was a shame. They whipped and they stripped and they hung me high, And they
4. I danced on a Fri-day when the sky turned black; It's hard to dance with the dev-il on your back. They bur-ied my bod-y and they thought I'd gone, But
5. They cut me down and I leap up high. I am the life that'll nev-er, nev-er die, I'll live in you if you'll live in me,

302 Eternal Life in Me

Warren Meyer and
Janet Bowser Manning

SANTA LUCIA
Arranged from Teodoro Cottrau

1. E - ter - nal life in me, Spark of di - vin-i-ty, Gives me a vi - tal glow And caus-es me to grow. E - ter - nal life in me, Stream of God's har-mo-ny, Is for - ev - er flow-ing, bless-ing me With pur - est en - er - gy.

2. E - ter - nal life in me, Breath of in - fin-i-ty, Quick-ens my heart and soul, Cleans-es and makes me whole. I am the Christ de - sign, Glo - ri - ous life di -vine! In me, through me, per-fect light may shine! E - ter - nal life is mine.

Now the Green Blade Riseth 303

FRENCH CAROL
Traditional French Carol, "Noël Nouvelet"
Harmonized by Martin Shaw 1875-1958

J. M. C. Crum 1872-1958

1. Now the green blade ris - eth from the bur - ied grain,
2. In the grave they laid Him, Love whom men had slain,
3. Forth He came at Eas - ter, like the ris - en grain,
4. When our hearts are win - try, griev - ing, or in pain,

Wheat that in dark earth man - y days has lain;
Think - ing that nev - er He would wake a - gain,
He that for three days in the grave had lain,
Thy touch can call us back to life a - gain,

Love lives a - gain, that with the dead has been:
Laid in the earth like grain that sleeps un - seen:
Quick from the dead my ris - en Lord is seen:
Fields of our hearts that dead and bare have been:

Refrain

Love is come a - gain like wheat that spring - eth green.

304   Spring Has Now Unwrapped the Flowers

The Oxford Book of Carols, 1928
Translation by Percy Dearmer

TEMPUS ADEST FLORIDUM
Piae Cantiones, 1582
Harmonization by John Stainer

1. Spring has now un-wrapped the flowers, Day is fast re-viv-ing,
2. Through each won-der of fair days God Him-self ex-press-es;
3. Praise the Mak-er, all ye saints; He with glo-ry girt you,

Life in all her grow-ing powers Towards the light is striv-ing;
Beau-ty fol-lows all His ways, As the world He bless-es;
He who skies and mead-ows paints Fash-ioned all your vir-tue;

All the world with beau-ty fills, Gold the green en-hanc-ing;
So, as He re-news the earth, Art-ist with-out ri-val,
Praise Him, se-ers, he-roes, kings, Her-alds of per-fec-tion;

Flowers make glee a-mong the hills, And set the mead-ows danc-ing.
In His grace of glad new birth We must seek re-vi-val.
Broth-ers, praise Him, for He brings All to res-ur-rec-tion!

For the Beauty of the Earth

DIX
Adapted from Conrad Kocher
by W. H. Monk

Folliott S. Pierpoint, adapted

1. For the beau - ty of the earth,
2. For the beau - ty of each hour
3. For the joy of ear and eye;
4. For the joy of hu - man love,

For the glo - ry of the skies, For the love which
Of the day and of the night, Hill and vale, and
For the heart and mind's de - light; For the mys - tic
Broth - er, sis - ter, par - ent, child; Love we praise all

from our birth O - ver and a - round us lies:
tree and flower, Sun and moon, and stars of light:
har - mo - ny Link - ing sense to sound and sight:
things a - bove; Gen - tle, peace - ful, calm, and mild:

Lord of all, to Thee we raise This our hymn of grate - ful praise.

306   Come, Ye Thankful People, Come

ST. GEORGE'S WINDSOR

Henry Alford, adapted

George J. Elvey

1. Come, ye thank-ful peo-ple, come, Raise the song of
2. All the world is God's own field, Fruit un-to His
3. For the Lord our God shall come, And shall take His

har-vest home; All is safe-ly gath-ered in,
praise to yield; Wheat and tares to-geth-er sown,
har-vest home; From His field shall in that day

Ere the win-ter storms be-gin; God, our Mak-er, doth pro-vide
Un-to joy or sor-row grown; First the blade, and then the ear,
All of-fens-es purge a-way; There, for-ev-er pu-ri-fied,

For our wants to be sup-plied; Come to God's own
Then the full corn shall ap-pear; Lord of har-vest,
In His pres-ence to a-bide— E-ven so, Lord,

As We're Sowing 307

JACOB'S LADDER
Traditional Spiritual

Christina Hovemann

tem - ple, come, Raise the song of har - vest home.
grant that we Whole-some grain and pure may be.
quick - ly come, Raise the glo - rious har - vest home.

1. As we're sow - ing, we are reap - ing, As we're
2. Sow - ing seeds of lov - ing - kind - ness, Sow - ing
3. Sow - ing now for bright to - mor - rows, Sow - ing

sow - ing, we are reap - ing, As we're sow - ing,
seeds of lov - ing - kind - ness, Sow - ing seeds of
now for bright to - mor - rows, Sow - ing now for

we are reap - ing, Chil - dren of the Light.
lov - ing - kind - ness, Chil - dren of the Light.
bright to - mor - rows, Chil - dren of the Light.

308

Bringing In the Sheaves

Knowles Shaw

MINOR
George A. Minor

1. Sow-ing in the morn - ing, sow-ing seeds of kind-ness,
2. Sow-ing in the sun - shine, sow-ing in the shad-ows,

Sow-ing in the noon - tide and the dew-y eve;
Fear-ing nei - ther clouds nor win-ter's chill-ing breeze;

Wait-ing for the har - vest, and the time of reap-ing,
By and by the har - vest, and the la - bor end - ed,

We shall come, re-joic - ing, bring-ing in the sheaves.
We shall come, re-joic - ing, bring-ing in the sheaves.

Refrain

Bring-ing in the sheaves, bring-ing in the sheaves,

We shall come, re - joic - ing, bring-ing in the sheaves;

Bring-ing in the sheaves, bring-ing in the sheaves,

We shall come, re -joic - ing, bring - ing in the sheaves.

309   Quiet Waters

Bill Provost   Bill Provost

1. Qui - et wa - ters all a - round me, Qui - et thoughts pre -
2. Vi - sions in my mind are clear - er, Draw - ing near - er

pare the way; Qui - et light a - glow with - in me,
ev - ery day; With each taste of sweet ful - fill - ment

Grow - ing bright - er as I pray.
I give thanks each time I pray.

Ev - er - know - ing

Mind to guide my way 'Til day is done.

310   We Thank You, Lord of Heaven

ABENDLIED
J. G. Ebeling
Jan Struther (1901–53)
Arranged by Martin Shaw (1875–1958)

1. We thank You, Lord of Heav - en, For all the joys that greet us, For all that You have giv - en To help us and de - light us In earth and sky and seas; The sun - light on the
2. For swift and gal - lant hors - es, For lambs in pas - tures spring - ing, For dogs with friend - ly fac - es, For birds with mu - sic throng - ing Their chan - tries in the trees; For herbs to cool our
3. For home - ly dwell - ing plac - es Where child-hood's vi - sions lin - ger, For friends and kind - ly voic - es, For bread to stay our hun - ger And sleep to bring us ease; For zeal and zest of

mead - ows, The rain-bow's fleet - ing won - der, The
fe - ver, For flowers of field and gar - den, For
liv - ing, For faith and un - der - stand - ing, For

clouds with cool - ing shad - ows, The stars that shine in
bees a - mong the clo - ver With sto - len sweet-ness
words to tell our lov - ing, For hope of peace un -

splen - dor — We thank You, Lord, for these.
lad - en — We thank You, Lord, for these.
end - ing — We thank You, Lord, for these.

311 Thank You, Father

Dennis Neagle

Dennis Neagle

1. Thank You, Fa-ther, for the joy of laugh-ter,
2. Thank You, Fa-ther, for the gift of be-ing,

Thank You, Fa-ther, for the love You bring.
Thank You, Fa-ther, for e - ter - ni - ty.

Thank You, Fa-ther, now and ev - er af - ter,
Thank You, Fa-ther, for this way of see-ing,

"Thank You, Fa-ther," is the song we sing.
Thank You, Fa-ther, for our u - ni-ty.

Used by permission of Dennis Neagle.

312 This Is My Thanksgiving Day

Carmen Moshier

Carmen Moshier

Slowly

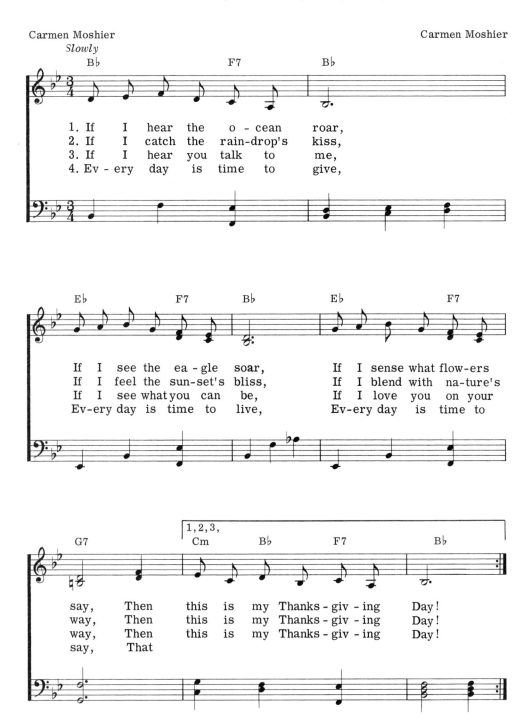

1. If I hear the o - cean roar,
2. If I catch the rain-drop's kiss,
3. If I hear you talk to me,
4. Ev - ery day is time to give,

If I see the ea - gle soar,
If I feel the sun-set's bliss,
If I see what you can be,
Ev-ery day is time to live,

If I sense what flow-ers
If I blend with na-ture's
If I love you on your
Ev-ery day is time to

say, Then this is my Thanks - giv - ing Day!
way, Then this is my Thanks - giv - ing Day!
way, Then this is my Thanks - giv - ing Day!
say, That

this is my Thanks-giv-ing Day, This is my Thanks-giv-ing Day, This is my Thanks-giv-ing Day!

313   We Gather Together

KREMSER
Netherlands Folk Song
Arranged by Edward Kremser

Selected

1. We gath-er to-geth-er to ask the Lord's bless-ing, In
2. With-in us a-bid-ing, our God, ev-er guid-ing, Or-
3. We come to sing prais-es with glad al-le-lu-ias, And

si-lence and serv-ice His will is now done. His
dain and main-tain Your true king-dom di-vine. As
know that in giv-ing our bless-ing shall be. Let

word ev-er stress-ing, His won-der ex-press-ing, Sing
from the be-gin-ning, the prize we are win-ning; O
this con-gre-ga-tion pro-claim the new cre-a-tion; In

prais-es to the Fa-ther, We know we are one!
Light, re-veal the way, O Love, in us shine.
Spir-it, we are one, In Christ, we are free!

He's Got the Whole World in His Hand   **314**

Traditional, adapted

Traditional Spiritual

1. He's got the whole world
2. He's got you and me, broth-er,
3. He's got my soul and bod-y

in His hand, He's got the whole world
in His hand, He's got you and me, sis-ter,
in His hand, He's got my soul and bod-y

in His hand, He's got the whole world
in His hand, He's got you and me, broth-er,
in His hand, He's got my soul and bod-y

in His hand, He's got the whole world in His hand.
in His hand, He's got the whole world in His hand.
in His hand, He's got the whole world in His hand.

315
I Live in God's Way

Unknown

BEAUTIFUL BLUE DANUBE
Tune: Johann Strauss, Jr.

1. I live in God's way, His Truth, His life; I'm
2. God bless-es me now in ev-ery way; I

free from all doubt, all fear, all strife. My words are of
know what to do and what to say. I live in a

love, of joy, of peace; I think of God's
world of per-fect health; The king-dom of

good that can-not cease. The pow-er of God is
heav-en is my wealth. I'm free to ex-press per-

mine to use; He gives me all good that I can
fec - tion now, For Christ with -in me has shown me

choose. I live in His love, in His Truth,
how; And on - ly the good do I see

and ex - press e - ter - nal youth.
ev -ery - where, in you, in me.

316 Where Two or More Are Gathered

Mildred Collins

Mildred Collins

1. Where two or more are gath-ered, there am I.
(2. When) pa - tient love ex - press-es, there am I.
(3. When) head to heart is kneel-ing, there am I.

Where two or more are gath-ered, there am I.
When prayer an - swers stress-es, there am I.
When thought is wed to feel - ing, there am I.

Where two or more are gath-ered in my name, there am
When broth-er bless-es broth-er in my na-ture, there am
With faith in God be - liev-ing that e - ter-ni - ty is

I.   Yes, there am I!   Yes, there am I! 2. When
I.   Yes, there am I!   Yes, there am I! 3. When
thine, Then, there am I!   Yes, there am

I! With faith in God be-liev-ing that e-ter-ni-ty is
thine, Then, there am I! Yes, there am I!

Going Forward 317

Warren Meyer   Warren Meyer

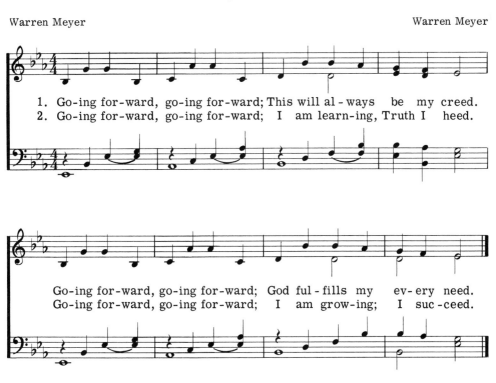

1. Go-ing for-ward, go-ing for-ward; This will al-ways be my creed.
2. Go-ing for-ward, go-ing for-ward; I am learn-ing, Truth I heed.

Go-ing for-ward, go-ing for-ward; God ful-fills my ev-ery need.
Go-ing for-ward, go-ing for-ward; I am grow-ing; I suc-ceed.

318   The Love Come A-Tricklin' Down

Anonymous   Traditional Spiritual

Refrain

Seek and ye shall find, Knock and the door shall be o-pen.

Ask and it shall be giv-en, and the love come a-trick-lin' down.

Unison

1. O yes, the Lord is pres-ent, O yes, the Lord is pres-ent,
2. O yes, the Lord is speak-ing, O yes, the Lord is speak-ing,
3. We're one in mind and spir-it, We're one in mind and spir-it,
4. I see the Christ with-in you, I see the Christ with-in you,

O yes, the
O yes, the
We're one in
I see the

Lord is pres - ent, and the love come a - trick - lin' down.
Lord is speak - ing, and the love come a - trick - lin' down.
mind and spir - it, and the love come a - trick - lin' down.
Christ with - in you, and the love come a - trick - lin' down.

Prayer Response   **319**

Anonymous   Anonymous

Now I whis-per, "Peace, be still," And for-ev-er trust God's will.

Now I whis-per, "Peace, be still." And for-ev-er trust God's will.

320 Namaskar

Mildred Collins

Mildred Collins

1. Na-mas-kar, I sa-lute the di-vin-i-ty in you. Na-mas-kar,
2. Na-mas-kar, Speak the word, help its truth and life to be. Na-mas-kar,

May my love help di-vin-i-ty shine through.
With God's na-ture in ev-ery man a-gree.

Fel-low man, re-veal God's plan.
Near, not far; God's hu-man star.

Namaskar is a Hindu word meaning, "I salute (or behold) the divinity in you."

Na-mas-kar, Na-mas-kar, Na-mas-kar!
Na-mas-kar, Na-mas-kar, Na-mas-kar!

We Are Climbing Jacob's Ladder 321

JACOB'S LADDER
Traditional Spiritual

Traditional Spiritual

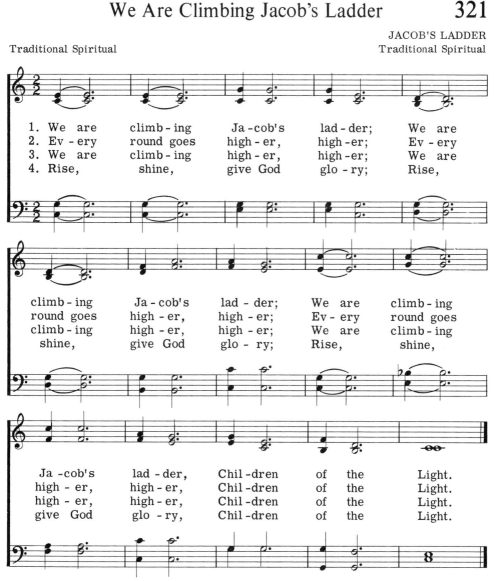

1. We are climb-ing Ja-cob's lad-der; We are
2. Ev-ery round goes high-er, high-er; Ev-ery
3. We are climb-ing high-er, high-er; We are
4. Rise, shine, give God glo-ry; Rise,

climb-ing Ja-cob's lad-der; We are climb-ing
round goes high-er, high-er; Ev-ery round goes
climb-ing high-er, high-er; We are climb-ing
shine, give God glo-ry; Rise, shine,

Ja-cob's lad-der, Chil-dren of the Light.
high-er, high-er, Chil-dren of the Light.
high-er, high-er, Chil-dren of the Light.
give God glo-ry, Chil-dren of the Light.

322   I Am Free, I Am Unlimited

Janet Bowser Manning   Janet Bowser Manning

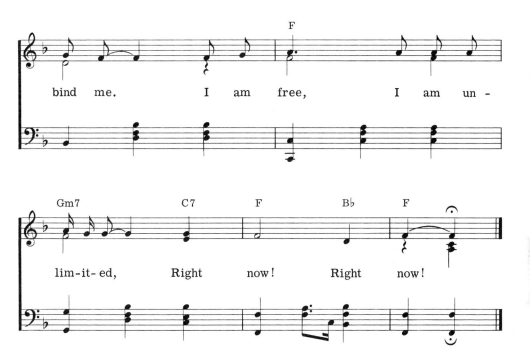

bind me.   I am free,   I am un -

lim-it- ed,   Right   now!   Right   now!

323 His Banner Over Me Is Love

Based on Psalm 23   Traditional

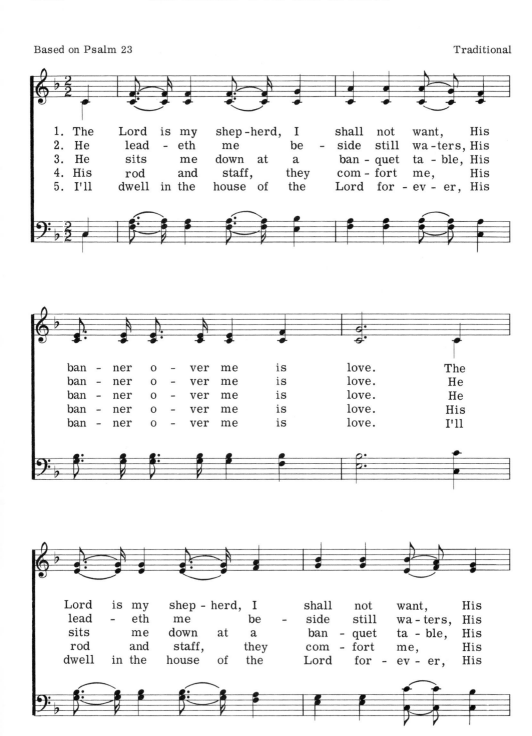

1. The Lord is my shep-herd, I shall not want, His
2. He lead-eth me be-side still wa-ters, His
3. He sits me down at a ban-quet ta-ble, His
4. His rod and staff, they com-fort me, His
5. I'll dwell in the house of the Lord for-ev-er, His

ban-ner o-ver me is love. The
ban-ner o-ver me is love. He
ban-ner o-ver me is love. He
ban-ner o-ver me is love. His
ban-ner o-ver me is love. I'll

Lord is my shep-herd, I shall not want, His
lead-eth me be-side still wa-ters, His
sits me down at a ban-quet ta-ble, His
rod and staff, they com-fort me, His
dwell in the house of the Lord for-ev-er, His

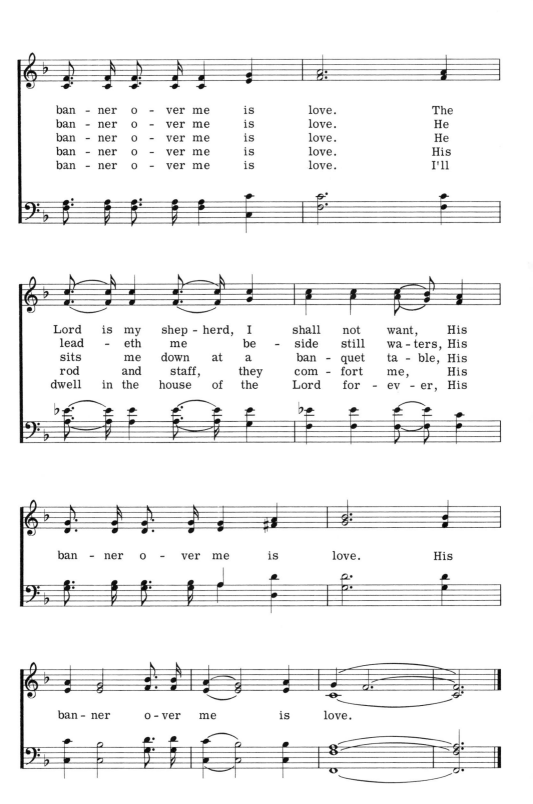

ban - ner o - ver me is love. The
ban - ner o - ver me is love. He
ban - ner o - ver me is love. He
ban - ner o - ver me is love. His
ban - ner o - ver me is love. I'll

Lord is my shep - herd, I shall not want, His
lead - eth me be - side still wa - ters, His
sits me down at a ban - quet ta - ble, His
rod and staff, they com - fort me, His
dwell in the house of the Lord for - ev - er, His

ban - ner o - ver me is love. His

ban - ner o - ver me is love.

324 Somethin's Up in the Universe

Janet Bowser Manning

Janet Bowser Manning

Some-thin's up in the u-ni-verse, You can feel it in the air! Some-thin's up in the u-ni-verse, You can hear it ev-ery-where. It sounds like laugh-ter (Ho! Ho! Ho!) And it feels like love (Hug Hug Hug). It's the

325 Praise Him, All Ye Little Children

Traditional   Traditional

1. Praise Him, praise Him, all ye lit-tle chil-dren,
2. Love Him, love Him, all ye lit-tle chil-dren,
3. Thank Him, thank Him, all ye lit-tle chil-dren,

God is love, God is love;
God is love, God is love;
God is love, God is love;

Praise Him, praise Him, all ye lit-tle chil-dren,
Love Him, love Him, all ye lit-tle chil-dren,
Thank Him, thank Him, all ye lit-tle chil-dren,

God is love, God is love.
God is love, God is love.
God is love, God is love.

I'm Gonna Sing

Traditional   Traditional

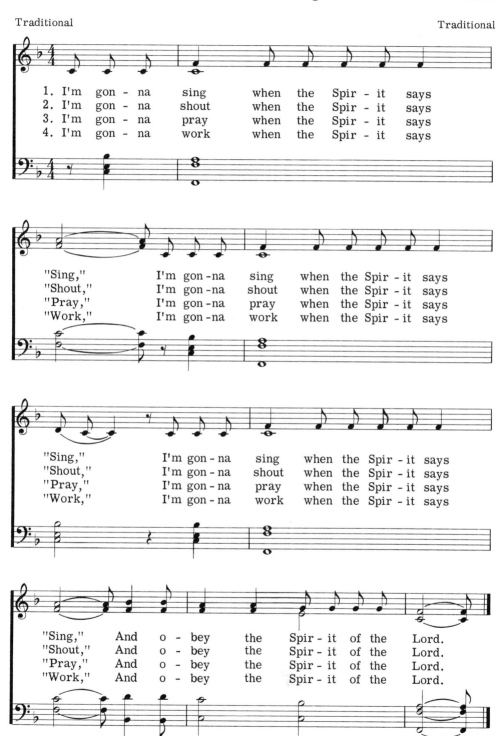

1. I'm gon - na sing when the Spir - it says
2. I'm gon - na shout when the Spir - it says
3. I'm gon - na pray when the Spir - it says
4. I'm gon - na work when the Spir - it says

"Sing," I'm gon -na sing when the Spir - it says
"Shout," I'm gon -na shout when the Spir - it says
"Pray," I'm gon -na pray when the Spir - it says
"Work," I'm gon -na work when the Spir - it says

"Sing," I'm gon - na sing when the Spir - it says
"Shout," I'm gon - na shout when the Spir - it says
"Pray," I'm gon - na pray when the Spir - it says
"Work," I'm gon - na work when the Spir - it says

"Sing," And o - bey the Spir - it of the Lord.
"Shout," And o - bey the Spir - it of the Lord.
"Pray," And o - bey the Spir - it of the Lord.
"Work," And o - bey the Spir - it of the Lord.

327   Ready

Warren Meyer   Warren Meyer

With vigor

1. I love
2. I give   be-cause it makes me read - y To
3. I sing
4. I pray

live the kind of life I'm seek - ing. When

I'm com-plete-ly u - ni-fied through   lov - ing,
       giv - ing,
       sing - ing,   The
       pray - ing,

whole wide world joins me and   loves.
       gives.
       sings.   I
       prays.

328   If You're Happy and You Know It

Traditional   Traditional

4. . . . nod your head! . . . 5. . . . say Amen! . . . 6. . . . do all five! . .

Note: Clap, stamp, etc. as each verse indicates.

God Is So Good

Unknown

Unknown

1. God is so good,
2. He heal - eth me,
3. He bless - es me,

God is so good,
He heal - eth me,
He bless - es me,

God is so good, He's so
God is so good, He
God is so good, He

good to me.
heal - eth me.
bless - es me.

330   Like the Father

Carl Frangkiser   Carl Frangkiser

1. I shall have on - ly thoughts of life, thoughts of
2. I shall have on - ly thoughts of joy, thoughts of

life, thoughts of life, All be - cause I am
joy, thoughts of joy, All be - cause I am

like my Fa - ther, Who is joy - ous life.
like my Fa - ther, Who is joy - ous life.

Refrain

Thoughts of life, thoughts of joy: I am

like my Fa - ther! Ev - ery girl, ev - ery

boy, Think - ing like the Fa - ther.

331   I Am Walking in the Light

Elizabeth Caspari
Verse 2, Anonymous

Traditional

1. I am *walk-ing in the light, In the light, in the light,
2. Oh, my good is ev-ery-where, ev-ery-where, ev-ery-where,

I am walk-ing in the light, In the light of God.
Oh, my good is ev-ery-where, Man-i-fest-ing now.

In the light, in the light, In the light, in the light,
O-ver here, o-ver there, With-in, with-out, ev-ery-where.

In the light, in the light, In the light of God.
Thank You, God, for my good, man-i-fest-ing now.

* Other words may be used: Happy; healthy; protected; prospered; guided; praying;
learning; working; playing; living.

Rejoice in the Lord Always

Traditional   Traditional

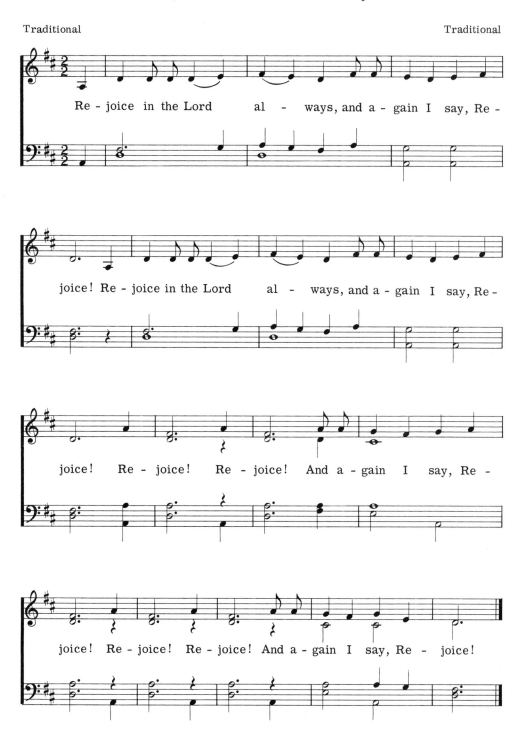

This song may be sung as a round, groups entering four measures apart.

333   Sing and Be Happy

Warren Meyer   Warren Meyer

Other words may be used: Smile, laugh, work, pray, play, etc.

Copyright 1976 in "Sing — Be Happy" by Warren Meyer. Used by permission.

Happy Little Children

LOVE SONG

Sadie M. Thomas, altered

Emory L. Coblentz

1. Hap - py lit - tle chil-dren, Hap - py all day long,
2. Hap - py lit - tle chil-dren, Hear our voic - es ring;
3. Hap - py lit - tle chil-dren, On this ho - ly day,
4. Love is for the us - ing; Let us show you how!

Do you know the se - cret Of our hap - py song?
Hap - py lit - tle chil-dren, Joy - ous - ly we sing.
Would you know the rea - son? Lis - ten what we say.
We can love each oth - er And we'll do it now.

Refrain Unison

L - O - V - E, love, L - O - V - E, love,

This is why we are so hap-py; L - O - V - E, love.

335 Why We're Happy

Roger Carl   Roger Carl

We will tell you in this song   Why we're hap-py all day long.

In our work and in our play   This is what we think each day:

Think-ing thoughts of kind - ness,   Think-ing thoughts of love;

Think-ing thoughts of kind - ness,   Think-ing thoughts of love.

When I Go A-Walking

Christiana Cronemeyer

Christiana Cronemeyer

When I go a-walk-ing and the sun is bright,

Then I go a-sing-ing, for my heart is light.

Sing a song of glad-ness all a-long the way;

God is ev-er with me, and will keep me through the day.

337 When You Rule Your Mind

Bill Provost

Bill Provost

1. Think light in the face of dark-ness;
(2. Think) high when you're feel - in' low - down;
(3. Think) life, full of vim and vig - or;

Think faith when you're lost at sea;
Think free when you want to fly;
Think truth, let the spir - it flow;

Think good, for there is no e - vil in the
Think big if you want to grow up in the
Think love, and there will be love in all the

world un - less you think there ought to be;
world; un - less you think, you'll nev - er try.
world; un - less you think, you'll nev - er know.

Note: This may be performed starting in C Major, raising the key $\frac{1}{2}$ step for each verse, ending with Verse 3 in D, as written.

338   'Tis the Gift to Be Simple

SIMPLE GIFTS
Traditional

Traditional Shaker Hymn

Unison

'Tis the gift to be sim-ple, 'tis the gift to be free, 'Tis the gift to come down where you ought to be, And when we find our - selves in the place just right, 'Twill be in the val - ley of love and de - light.

339   Wonderful Child

Cris Colombo

Cris Colombo
Arrangement by Jim Bestman

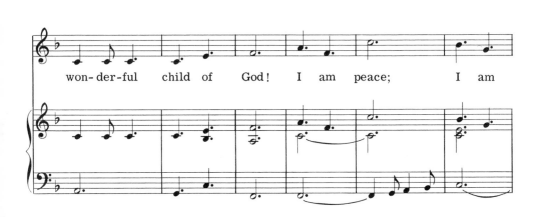

I am so won-der-ful; I am so won-der-ful; I am a won-der-ful child of God! I am so won-der-ful; I am so won-der-ful; I am a won-der-ful child of God!

Additional verses may be:

2. You are love; you are joy; You are a wonderful child of God....
3. Each is love; each is joy; Each is a wonderful child of God....

340   Joy in My Heart

George W. Cooke   George W. Cooke

1. I have the joy, joy, joy, joy,
2. I have the peace that pass - eth un - der - stand - ing

Down in my heart, Down in my heart,
Down in my heart, Down in my heart,

Down in my heart; I have the joy, joy, joy, joy,
Down in my heart; I have the peace that pass-eth un-der-stand-ing

Down in my heart, Down in my heart to stay.
Down in my heart, Down in my heart to stay.

Love the Good You See in All

341

Lydia Gardiner Worth

Ernst Krohr

1. Love is gen-tle, love is sweet, Love has will-ing hands and feet.
2. Love is nev-er cross and rude; Love is ev-er kind and good.

Love your work and love your play, Love the Lord of ev-ery day;
Love makes hap-py, smil-ing fac-es, Let it shine in all dark plac-es!

Love the birds and love the flowers, Love the fresh, sweet morn-ing hours.
Wheth-er great or wheth-er small, Love the good you see in all;

Al-ways love to do your part, Then you'll have a hap-py heart.
Wheth-er great or wheth-er small, Love the good you see in all.

342

Hallelu, Hallelu

Unknown

Unknown

Hal-le-lu, hal-le-lu, hal-le-lu, hal-le-lu-jah; Praise ye the Lord!

Hal-le-lu, hal-le-lu, hal-le-lu, hal-le-lu-jah; Praise ye the Lord!

Praise ye the Lord! Hal-le-lu-jah; Praise ye the Lord! Hal-le-lu-jah;

Praise ye the Lord! Hal-le-lu-jah; Praise ye the Lord!

I Feel Wonderful

Ruth Peale

Adapted from Charles H. Gabriel

1. I feel won-der-ful, I feel won-der-ful
2. You look won-der-ful, you look won-der-ful

For this is a glo-rious day,
For this is a glo-rious day,

I feel won-der-ful, I feel won-der-ful,
You look won-der-ful, you look won-der-ful,

And I'm go-ing to stay that way.
And you are go-ing to stay that way.

344　There Is Joy in My Heart

Mildred Collins

Mildred Collins

There is joy in my heart and a smile on my face 'cause I love the world. There's a song on my lips, love the whole hu-man race, and I love the world. Feel my

345   I Am So Happy

Anonymous

Warren Meyer

I am so hap-py, per-pet-ual-ly hap-py! Oh!

I am so hap-py and free!

Sum-mer-time, win-ter-time, spring-time, and au-tumn, Yes!

I am so hap-py and free! In-side me, out-side me,

346 I'm Ready for a Miracle

Carmen Moshier

Carmen Moshier

347

O It's Great

The Lord Is My Shepherd

348

Traditional

Traditional Melody

1. The Lord is my shep-herd, I'll walk with Him al - ways.

2. Be - side the still wa -ters I'll walk with Him al - ways.

Al - ways, al - ways, I'll walk with Him al - ways. Al -

ways, al - ways, I'll walk with Him al - ways.

To sing as a round, the new group should begin at 1. when the preceding group reaches 2.

349 The Song of the Universe

Carmen Moshier
Based on poem by J. Sig Paulson

Carmen Moshier

1. The u-ni-verse sings   I AM, I AM!

The u-ni-verse rings   I AM, I AM!

The u-ni-verse brings   through each at-om and cell

a song of its own: it's sing-ing I AM.

* For ending, "Sing the universe song: I AM, I AM!" may be sung 3 times.

350 The Happy Song

Carmen Moshier

Carmen Moshier

Hap - py am I to - day; This is my hap - py day. Hap - py am I to - day; This is my hap - py day!

1. All sing "The Happy Song," followed by "The Good Song." (See next page.)

2. Combine the two songs, one group singing "The Happy Song" while another group sings "The Good Song." (Raise the key to F Major.)

3. Reverse groups singing "The Happy Song" and "The Good Song." (Raise the key again, to G Major.)

The Good Song

Carmen Moshier   Carmen Moshier

I am one with good that's meant for me.

Good you may not see, but still it's meant for me.

I am one with good that's meant for me,

Good that's meant for me to - day!

352   I Am in Harmony

Mildred Collins   Mildred Collins

I am in har-mo-ny, I am in har-mo-ny,

Al - ways se - cure and free, With the rhy-thm of the

u - ni-verse. I am in har-mo-ny, I am in

har - mo- ny, Al - ways se-cure and free, With the

rhy-thm of the u-ni-verse, *(clap - clap - clap - clap)* With the

rhy-thm of the u-ni-verse, *(clap - clap - clap - clap)* With the

rhy-thm of the u-ni-verse, *(clap - clap - clap - clap)* With the

rhy-thm of *(clap - clap)* the u-ni-verse! *(clap - clap)*

353

Guess What

Bill Provost

Bill Provost

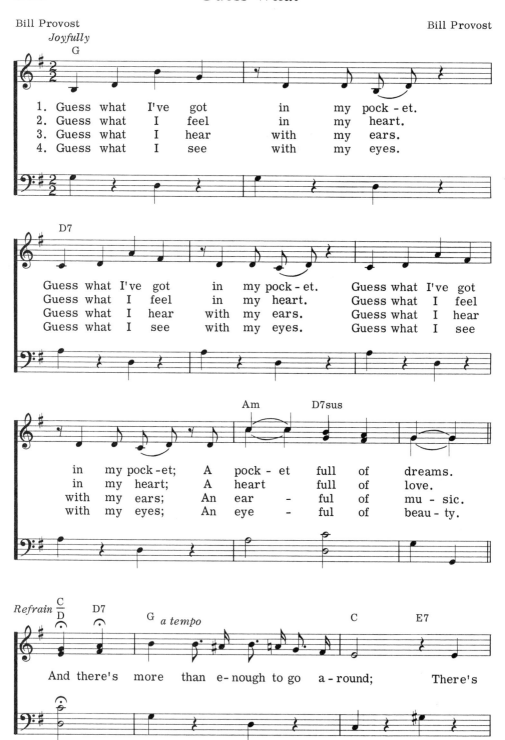

Joyfully

1. Guess what I've got in my pock-et.
2. Guess what I feel in my heart.
3. Guess what I hear with my ears.
4. Guess what I see with my eyes.

Guess what I've got in my pock-et. Guess what I've got
Guess what I feel in my heart. Guess what I feel
Guess what I hear with my ears. Guess what I hear
Guess what I see with my eyes. Guess what I see

in my pock-et; A pock-et full of dreams.
in my heart; A heart full of love.
with my ears; An ear-ful of mu-sic.
with my eyes; An eye-ful of beau-ty.

Refrain *a tempo*

And there's more than e-nough to go a-round; There's

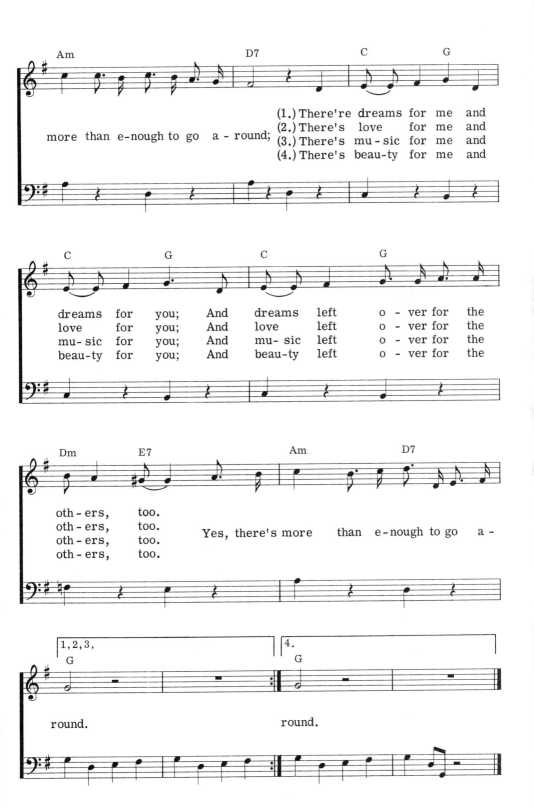

354 It's Love That Makes the World Go 'Round

Traditional

Traditional

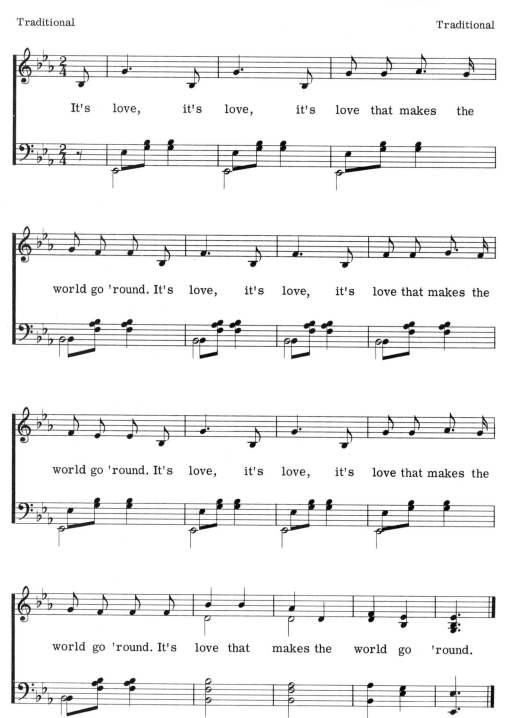

God's Love Is Deep Within Me

355

SWING LOW SWEET CHARIOT
American Folk Hymn

Anonymous

1. God's love is deep with-in me,

Ev-er sat-is-fy-ing my soul.

God's love is deep with-in me,

Ev-er sat-is-fy-ing my soul.

2. God's life is deep within me . . .

3. God's light is deep within me . . .

I've Got Peace Like a River

Traditional, adapted

Traditional Melody

peace   like   a   riv - er,   I've   got   peace   like   a
love   like   a   moun-tain,   I've   got   love   like   a
joy   like   a   foun -tain,   I've   got   joy   like   a

riv - er   in   my   soul!
moun - tain   in   my   soul!
foun - tain   in   my   soul!

357   Miracles Are Happening

Betty Butterworth and
Wilma Powell

Based on melody by Edvard Grieg

Eye hath not seen, and ear hath not heard, The

good that God has for me. My

mind is now o - pen, my heart is re - cep - tive, And

mira - cles are happen -ing to me. Oh!

358   I Love Unity

Bill Provost   Bill Provost

1. Ev-ery-bod-y is sing-ing in U-ni-ty, Ev-ery-one has got a mel-o-dy; When you're tuned to Source, You are on the course;
2. Ev-ery-bod-y is wel-come in U-ni-ty, Ev-ery-one is per-fect, whole, and free; God is all a-round, Love and Truth a-bound,
3. Ev-ery-bod-y is hap-py in U-ni-ty, Ev-ery-one is hap-py as can be; God is ev-ery-where With His love to share;

359   We Make Our Own World

Carmen Moshier

Carmen Moshier

Medium tempo, briskly

We make our own world, wher- ev-er we are,

Our hap-pi - ness is of our own mak - ing.

We make our own world, wher - ev-er we are,

Our hap-pi - ness then is for the tak - ing.

Our world goes with us as we talk and walk a - long each

360   God of Our Fathers

NATIONAL HYMN

Daniel C. Roberts, altered

George W. Warren

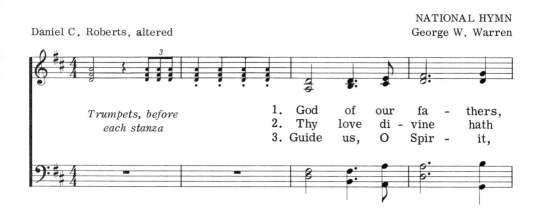

Trumpets, before
each stanza

1. God of our fa - thers,
2. Thy love di - vine hath
3. Guide us, O Spir - it,

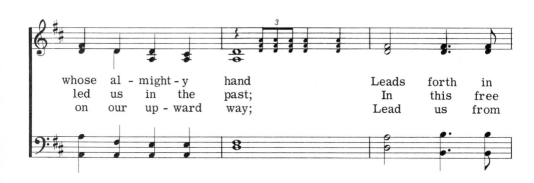

whose al - might-y hand   Leads forth in
led us in the past;   In this free
on our up - ward way;   Lead us from

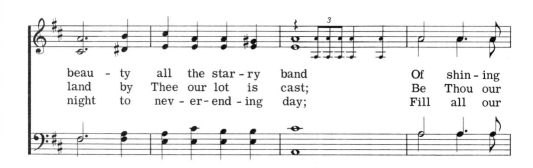

beau - ty all the star-ry band   Of shin - ing
land by Thee our lot is cast;   Be Thou our
night to nev - er-end-ing day;   Fill all our

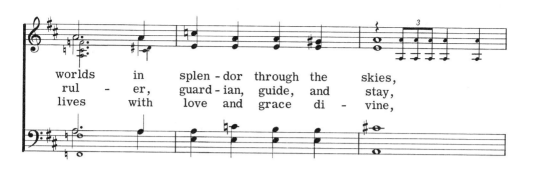

worlds | in | splen - dor | through | the | skies,
rul | - er, | guard - ian, | guide, | and | stay,
lives | with | love | and | grace | di - vine,

Our | grate - ful | songs | be - fore | Thy | throne | a - rise.
Thy | Word our | law, | Thy | paths our | cho - sen | way.
And | glo - ry, | laud, | and | praise be | ev - er | Thine.

361   The Star-Spangled Banner

Francis Scott Key

STAR-SPANGLED BANNER
Attributed to John Stafford Smith

1. O say, can you see, by the dawn's ear - ly light,
2. O thus be it ev - er when free men shall stand

What so proud - ly we hailed at the twi-light's last gleam-ing?
Be - tween their loved homes and the war's des - o - la - tion;

Whose broad stripes and bright stars, through the per - il - ous fight,
Blest with vic - tory and peace, may the heaven-res-cued land

O'er the ram-parts we watched, were so gal-lant-ly stream-ing.
Praise the Power that has made and pre-served us a na-tion.

362 O Beautiful for Spacious Skies

Katharine Lee Bates

MATERNA
Samuel A. Ward

1. O beau - ti - ful for spa - cious skies, For am - ber waves of grain, For pur - ple moun - tain maj - es - ties A - bove the fruit - ed plain!

2. O beau - ti - ful for pil - grim feet, Whose stern, im - pas - sioned stress A thor - ough-fare for free - dom beat A - cross the wil - der - ness!

3. O beau - ti - ful for he - roes proved In lib - er - at - ing strife, Who more than self their coun - try loved, And mer - cy more than life!

4. O beau - ti - ful for pa - triot dream That sees be - yond the years Thine al - a - bas - ter cit - ies gleam, Un - dimmed by hu - man tears!

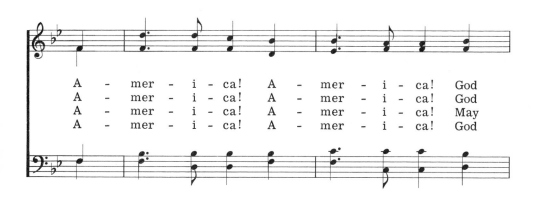

A - mer - i - ca! A - mer - i - ca! God
A - mer - i - ca! A - mer - i - ca! God
A - mer - i - ca! A - mer - i - ca! May
A - mer - i - ca! A - mer - i - ca! God

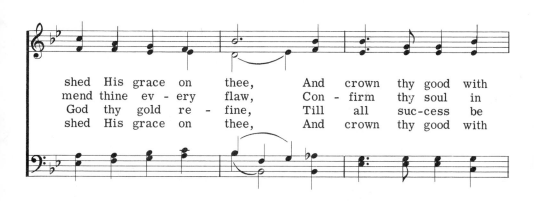

shed His grace on thee, And crown thy good with
mend thine ev - ery flaw, Con - firm thy soul in
God thy gold re - fine, Till all suc - cess be
shed His grace on thee, And crown thy good with

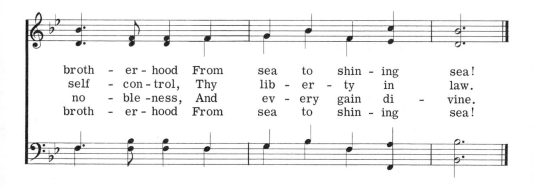

broth - er - hood From sea to shin - ing sea!
self - con - trol, Thy lib - er - ty in law.
no - ble - ness, And ev - ery gain di - vine.
broth - er - hood From sea to shin - ing sea!

363   Mine Eyes Have Seen the Glory

BATTLE HYMN OF THE REPUBLIC

Julia Ward Howe, adapted

William Steffe

1. Mine eyes have seen the glo - ry of the
2. He has sound - ed forth the trum - pet that shall
3. In the beau - ty of the lil - ies Christ was

com - ing of the Lord; He is tram-pling out the vin-tage where the
nev - er call re-treat; He is sift - ing out the hearts of men be-
born a - cross the sea, With a glo - ry in His bos-om that trans-

grapes of wrath are stored; He hath loosed the fate - ful light-ning of His
fore His judg-ment seat; O be swift, my soul, to an - swer him; be
fig - ures you and me; As He lived to make men ho - ly, let us

ter - ri - ble swift sword; His truth is march- ing on.
ju - bi - lant, my feet! Our God is march- ing on.
live to make men free! While God is march- ing on.

Refrain

Glo - ry! glo - ry! Hal - le - lu - jah! Glo - ry! glo - ry! Hal - le - lu - jah! Glo - ry! glo - ry! Hal - le - lu - jah! His truth is march - ing on.

364   My Country, 'Tis of Thee

AMERICA

Samuel F. Smith

Anonymous in *Thesaurus Musicus*, 1744

1. My coun-try, 'tis of thee, Sweet land of lib-er-ty,
2. My na-tive coun-try, thee, Land of the no-ble, free,
3. Let mu-sic swell the breeze, And ring from all the trees
4. Our fa-thers' God, to Thee, Au-thor of lib-er-ty,

Of thee I sing; Land where my fa-thers died,
Thy name I love; I love thy rocks and rills,
Sweet free-dom's song; Let mor-tal tongues a-wake;
To Thee we sing; Long may our land be bright

Land of the pil-grims' pride, From ev-ery
Thy woods and tem-pled hills; My heart with
Let all that breathe par-take; Let rocks their
With free-dom's ho-ly light; Pro-tect us

moun-tain-side Let free-dom ring!
rap-ture thrills, Like that a-bove.
si-lence break, The sound pro-long.
by Thy might, Great God, our King.

God Is My Bread of Life

BREAD OF LIFE

Warren Meyer

William F. Sherwin

1. God is my bread of life, Sub - stance in - deed;
2. God is my ho - ly life, E - ter - nal stream;
3. God shares His life with me That I may live;

When I com - mune with Him, He feeds my need.
I drink the cup of joy, His power su - preme.
His ac - tive love in me Is mine to give.

My mind and bod - y rest, They are as - sured;
My mind and bod - y rise, Di - vine - ly stirred;
Let si - lence rule my heart, His voice be heard;

They are se - cure in Christ, His liv - ing Word.
I feel the wave of Truth, His liv - ing Word.
Let all my be - ing know His liv - ing Word.

Words used by permission of Warren Meyer.

366 Break Thou the Bread of Life

Mary A. Lathbury
Verse 3, Anonymous

BREAD OF LIFE
William F. Sherwin

1. Break Thou the bread of life, Dear Lord, to me,
2. Bless Thou the truth, dear Lord, To me, to me,
3. As now I seek the Christ, Clear - ly I see,

As Thou didst break the loaves Be - side the sea.
As Thou didst bless the bread By Gal - i - lee;
And I give thanks for Truth Re - vealed to me.

Be - yond the sa - cred page I seek Thee, Lord;
Then shall all bond - age cease, All fet - ters fall;
My mind is filled with light, My heart is pure,

My spir - it pants for Thee, O liv - ing Word!
And I shall find my peace, My All in All.
For now at last I know The way is sure.

Father Eternal

HOW CAN I LEAVE THEE
Friedrich Kücken

Hannah More Kohaus

from Pluma M. Brown's *Song Hymnal*, 1897

1. Fa - ther e - ter - nal, Life pure and un - de -filed,
2. Fa - ther su - per - nal, Thou nev - er - fail - ing Love,
3. Fa - ther Al - might - y, Swift - ly our souls a - rise

Food for the rec - on - ciled, O liv - ing bread!
Com - ing from realms a - bove, O liv - ing bread!
To that which sat - is - fies, O liv - ing bread!

Bread with all sub-stance rife, Heal - ing all pain and strife,
Bread with all whole-ness fraught, Fra - grant with ho - ly thought,
Ra - diant its light shall be, Shin - ing e - ter -nal - ly,

Breath of e - ter - nal Life, O liv - ing bread!
On an -gels' pin - ions brought, O liv - ing bread!
With us in u - ni - ty, O liv - ing bread!

368 Prayer of Blessing

Janet Bowser Manning

AR HYD Y NOS
Traditional Welsh Melody

Pre - cious child, may peace at - tend you All through your life.

May you feel the love we send you All through your life.

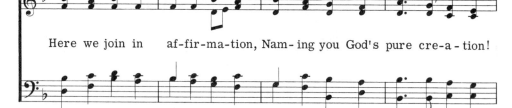

Here we join in af-fir-ma-tion, Nam- ing you God's pure cre-a-tion!

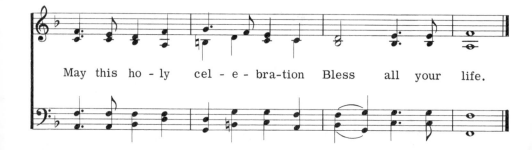

May this ho - ly cel - e - bra-tion Bless all your life.

Blessed Savior, We Pray

LULLABY
Johannes Brahms

Anonymous

Bless-ed Sav-ior, we pray, Bless this dear one this day.

Keep her/him ev-er near to Thee, And her/his life pure and free.

Bless-ed Lord, hear our prayer: May she/he rest in Thy care;

Bless-ed Lord, hear our prayer: May she/he live in Thy care.

370   Lord, Bless This House

James Dillet Freeman

MELITA
John B. Dykes

1. Lord, bless this house and bless us all In care and pleas-ure,
2. Lord, make my house a man-sion of A-bid-ing love-li-
3. Blest be these rooms for work or play! Oh, let my house be

great or small; Blest be the door friends en-ter by And
ness and love, A friend-ly, com-fort-a-ble place. Let
some-times gay And some-times still as can-dle-light. Be

win-dows that let in the sky, And roof a-bove and
pleas-ant talk like fire-light grace These rooms, and may friends
with us, Lord, both day and night; In care and pleas-ure,

walls a-bout That shut the world and weath-er out!
lin-ger long To join in laugh-ter or a song.
great or small, Lord, bless this house and bless us all!

God Lives with Me

CANONBURY

William H. Frazier

Arranged from Robert A. Schumann

1. God lives with me my home to bless With
2. His bless-ing rests up - on the walls, The

peace and love and hap - pi - ness; His
base - ment, at - tic, floors, and halls; My

pres - ence dwells in ev - ery room, And
cup - boards full shall ev - er be, For

thoughts of love re - place all gloom.
God Him - self is bless - ing me.

372 Glory Be to the Father

Henry W. Greatorex

Glo - ry be to the Fa - ther, and to the

Son, and to the Ho - ly Ghost; As it was in the be -

gin - ning, is now, and ev - er shall be,

world with - out end. A - men. A - men.

The Lord's Prayer

Gregorian

Unison

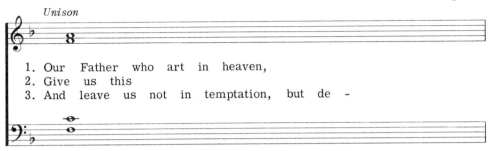

1. Our Father who art in heaven,
2. Give us this
3. And leave us not in temptation, but de -

hal - lowed be Thy name.
day our dai - ly bread;
liv - er us from evil;

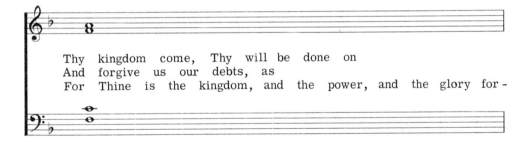

Thy kingdom come, Thy will be done on
And forgive us our debts, as
For Thine is the kingdom, and the power, and the glory for-

earth as it is in heaven.
we have for - given our debtors.
ev - er. A - men.

374 Let the Words of My Mouth

From Psalm 19

Adolph Baumbach

Let the words of my mouth, and the med-i-ta-tion of my heart be ac-cept-a-ble in Thy sight, O Lord, my strength and my Re-deem-er.

(Fine)

(Optional Ending)

O Lord, my strength, O Lord, my strength and my Re-

deem - er, O Lord, my strength, O Lord, my

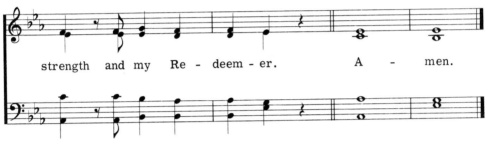

strength and my Re - deem - er. A - men.

The Lord's Prayer 375

Our Father who art in heaven, Hallowed be thy name.
Thy kingdom come.
Thy will be done in earth, as it is in heaven.
Give us this day our daily bread.
And forgive us our debts, as we also have forgiven our debtors.
And leave us not in temptation, but deliver us from evil.
For thine is the kingdom, and the power, and the glory,
     for ever.
Amen.

As prayed by Charles Fillmore, cofounder of Unity School of Christianity.

376

Invocation

Charles Fillmore

Warren Meyer

I am now in the pres-ence of pure Be - ing,
and im - mersed in the Ho - ly Spir - it of
life, love, and wis - dom. I ac - knowl - edge Thy
pres-ence and Thy pow - er, O bless-ed Spir - it.

Music used by permission of Warren Meyer

In Thy di-vine wis-dom now e-rase my mor-tal lim-i-ta-tions, and from Thy pure sub-stance of love bring in-to man-i-fes-ta-tion my world, ac-cord-ing to Thy per-fect law.

Twelve Powers
(Affirmations)

Bill Provost

Bill Provost

I. Faith

Christ through faith a - wak-ens in me now;

Christ through faith a - wak-ens in me now;

Christ through faith a - wak-ens in me now;

Note: This accompaniment is to be used for all "Twelve Powers."

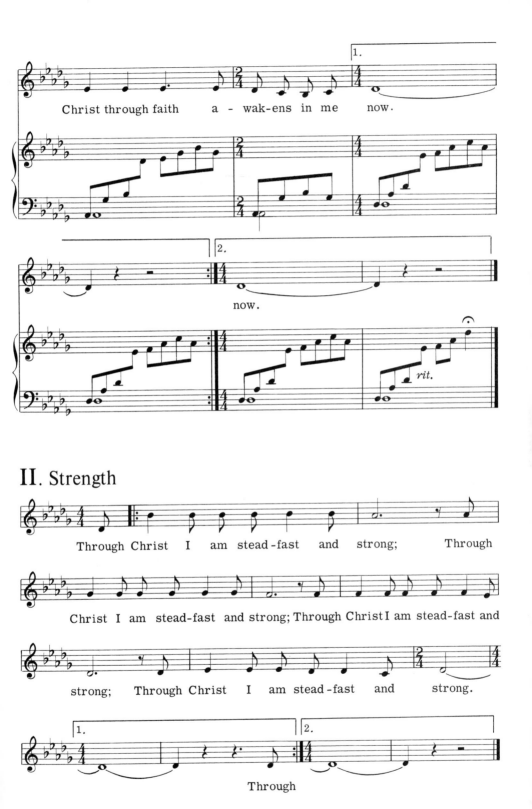

Christ through faith a - wak-ens in me now.

now.

rit.

II. Strength

Through Christ I am stead-fast and strong; Through

Christ I am stead-fast and strong; Through Christ I am stead-fast and

strong; Through Christ I am stead-fast and strong.

Through

III. Love

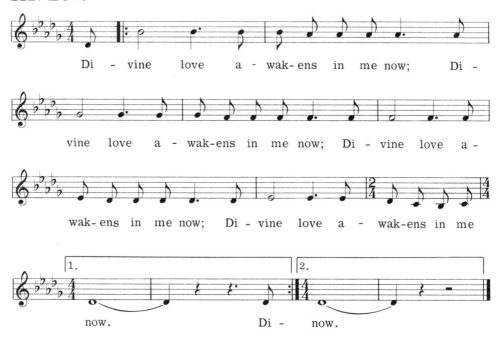

Di - vine love a - wak-ens in me now; Di -
vine love a - wak-ens in me now; Di - vine love a -
wak-ens in me now; Di - vine love a - wak-ens in me

1. now. Di - now.
2.

IV. Power

God's gift of pow - er quick-ens in me now;
God's gift of pow - er quick-ens in me now; God's gift of pow-er
quick-ens in me now; God's gift of pow - er quick-ens in me

1. now.
2. now.

V. Imagination

God's im - ag - i - na - tion   quick -ens   in   me now;

God's im-ag- i- na -tion quick-ens in me now; God's im-ag- i-na-tion

quick-ens in me now;   God's im - ag -i - na - tion   quick -ens in me

1.
now.

2.
now.

VI. Understanding

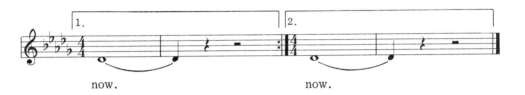

God's   un - der-stand - ing   quick -ens   in   me   now;

God's un-der-stand -ing quick -ens in me now; God's un-der-stand-ing

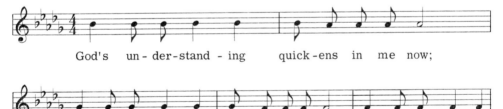

quick-ens in me now;   God's un - der -stand -ing   quick -ens in me

1.
now.

2.
now.

VII. Judgment

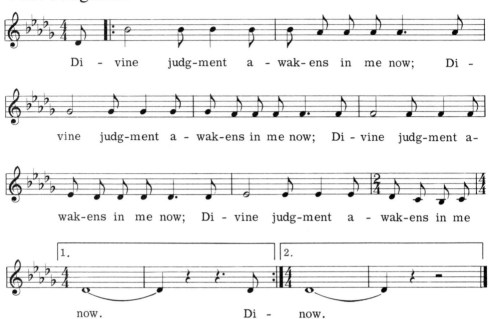

Di - vine judg-ment a - wak-ens in me now; Di -
vine judg-ment a - wak-ens in me now; Di - vine judg-ment a-
wak-ens in me now; Di - vine judg-ment a - wak-ens in me
now. Di - now.

VIII. Will

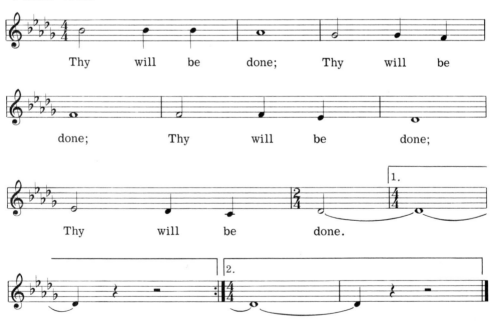

Thy will be done; Thy will be
done; Thy will be done;
Thy will be done.

IX. Order

Di - vine or -der a - wak-ens in me now; Di -

vine or-der a - wak-ens in me now; Di - vine or-der a -

wak-ens in me now; Di - vine or-der a - wak-ens in me

1.
now.

2.
Di - now.

X. Zeal

God's gift of zeal quick - ens in me now;

God's gift of zeal quick -ens in me now; God's gift of zeal

quick -ens in me now; God's gift of zeal quick- ens in me

1.
now.

2.
now.

XI. Renunciation

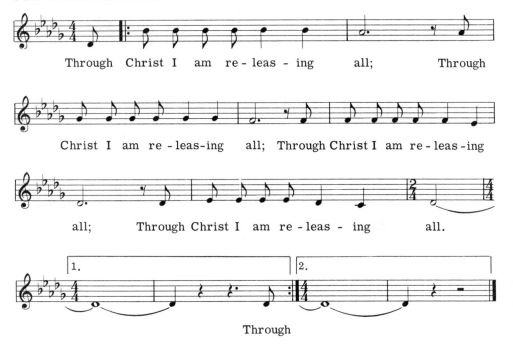

Through Christ I am re - leas - ing all; Through

Christ I am re - leas-ing all; Through Christ I am re - leas-ing

all; Through Christ I am re - leas - ing all.

1.

2.

Through

XII. Life

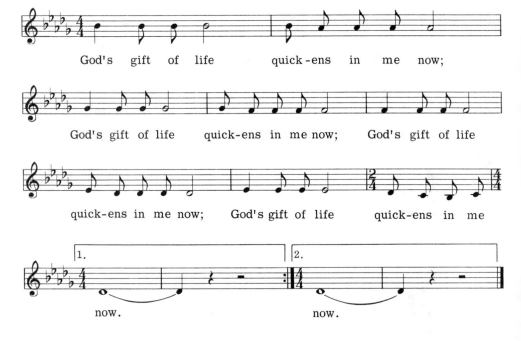

God's gift of life quick-ens in me now;

God's gift of life quick-ens in me now; God's gift of life

quick-ens in me now; God's gift of life quick-ens in me

1.

2.

now.

now.

Offering Song

Francis J. Gable

Carl Frangkiser

1. I give my of - fer - ing to God Be -
2. I trust in God for all my good, He
3. I give the la - bor of my hand, The

cause He gives to me. I praise and bless it
is my rich sup - ply. My gift is blessed with
thoughts of mind and heart; And so in all the

with His love, From lack I set it free.
love di - vine That it may mul - ti - ply.
Fa - ther's work I have a hap - py part.

Refrain

I give in love, my gift I bless, And giv-ing brings me hap-pi-ness.

379   Thanks Be to God

Grace

Bill Provost

Bill Provost

* Other words may be: peace; joy; love.

381 The Lord Bless You and Keep You

BENEDICTION
Peter C. Lutkin

From Numbers 6:24-26

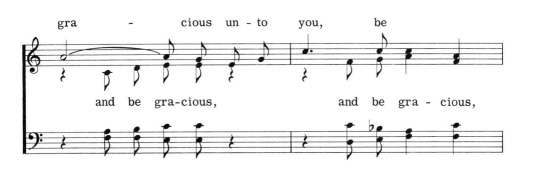

gra - cious un - to you, be

and be gra-cious, and be gra - cious,

The Lord be gra-cious, gra - cious

un - to you. A - men.

382 The Lord Bless You and Keep You

Numbers 6:24-26

Pluma M. Brown

The Lord bless you and keep you: The Lord make His face shine up - on you, and be gra - cious un - to you: The Lord lift up His coun - te - nance up - on you, and give you peace.

God Be with You Till We Meet Again   383

GOD BE WITH YOU

Adapted from Jeremiah E. Rankin

William G. Tomer

1. God be with you till we meet a - gain;
2. God be with you till we meet a - gain;

By His coun - sels guide, up - hold you,
Keep love's ban - ner float - ing o'er you;

In His love se - cure - ly fold you;
It will com - fort and pro - tect you;

God be with you till we meet a - gain.
God be with you till we meet a - gain.

384   Twofold Amen

Dresden

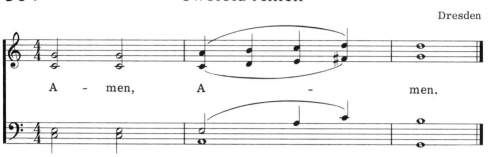

385   Threefold Amen

Danish

386   Fourfold Amen

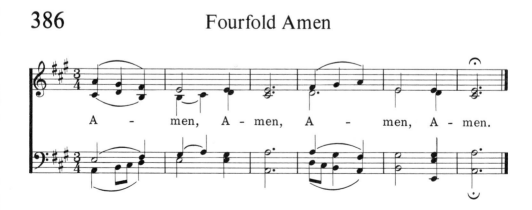

Fourfold Amen

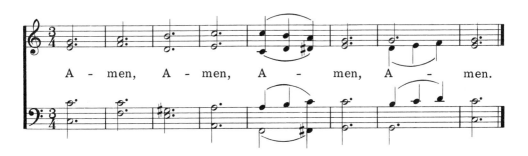

A - men, A - men, A - men, A - men.

Sevenfold Amen

John Stainer

Responsive
Readings

Spiritual Communion Responsive Reading

Purification (Personal forgiveness opportunity)   **1**

Leader: *"This is my commandment, that you love one another as I have loved you." (John 15:12)*

Response: The forgiving love of Jesus Christ cleanses me of all past mistakes. I AM whole and free! As I fully and freely forgive myself and others, so in turn am I fully and freely forgiven.

Spiritual Nourishment   **2**

Leader: *"Take, eat; this is my body." (Matt. 26:26)*

Response: I take in the bread of life. I AM filled with the radiant, living substance of Christ. I AM whole in mind and body. My mind and heart are filled with the Truth of Christ.

Leader: *And he took a cup, and when he had given thanks he gave it to them, saying, "Drink of it, all of you." (Matt. 26:27)*

Response: I AM filled with the new wine of Spirit. My mind and heart are renewed by the revitalizing power of Christ love.

Leader: *"Christ in you, the hope of glory." (Col. 1:27) "You will know the truth, and the truth will make you free." (John 8:32)*

Response: In faith and gratitude, I rededicate and reconsecrate myself to the will and the work of Jesus Christ, and to the unfoldment of my Christ nature.

Inner-Dependence: A Responsive Reading   **3**

Leader: *Today, as we celebrate the gift of freedom, let us remember that true freedom begins within. As we become still, we allow the presence of the indwelling Christ to fill every cell and fiber of our being. We look within, becoming one with this Christ presence, expressing through each of us in the power of the I AM.*

Response: I AM one with the Christ presence, whose light now fills my entire being.

Leader: *I let go the bonds of human limitation, and open wide the doors to infinite possibilities, as I allow the Christ to work through me.*

Response: My heart and mind are now willing to follow the Christ in all things.

Leader: *Truth flows through me in mighty currents, washing away doubt and fear. I attune myself to God's will in all that I AM.*

Response: I AM the Truth in living expression.

Leader: *"You will know the truth, and the truth will make you free." (John 8:32) I experience the power of these words and rejoice that I AM free to be the child of God's love I AM meant to be.*

Response: I AM a child of God—free and unlimited in my celebration of life.

Leader: *My declaration of inner-dependence flows through me as I allow these words to become living truths within me. Gently and prayerfully I repeat this personal declaration of inner-dependence silently: "I hold these Truths to be self-evident. I AM created free and equal, endowed by a loving Creator with the inalienable rights of a fulfilling life, the freedom of Christ-directed choices, and the experience of happiness every day of my life."*

Response: I affirm my declaration of inner-dependence now, seeking always to go first to God before taking any outer actions.

Leader: *"You will know the truth, and the truth will make you free." (John 8:32)*

Response: I know the Truth, and I AM free! Thank You, God!

4   Thanksgiving Responsive Prayer

Thinking Good Is Thanking God

Leader: *"Blessed are those who hunger and thirst for righteousness, for they shall be satisfied." (Matt. 5:6)*

Response: I AM open and receptive to God in prayer. I AM empty of fear and doubt, ready to be filled anew with wisdom and strength. Praise God!

Leader: *"Therefore do not be anxious, saying, 'What shall we eat?' or 'What shall we drink?' or 'What shall we wear?' . . . your heavenly Father knows that you need them all. But seek first his kingdom and his righteousness, and all these things shall be yours as well." (Matt. 6:31-33)*

Response: God is my instant, constant, abundant supply. I place God first in my life and I am fulfilled. Praise God!

Leader: *And taking the five loaves and the two fish he looked up to heaven, and blessed, and broke the loaves, and gave them to the disciples to set before the people; and he divided the two fish among them all. And they all ate and were satisfied. And they took up twelve baskets full of broken pieces and of the fish. And those who ate the loaves were five thousand men. (Mark 6:41-44)*

Response: The Christ indwelling sustains me always. I AM lovingly and abundantly supplied in the right way, and at the perfect time. Praise God!

Leader: *And Jesus answered them, "Have faith in God. Truly, I say to you, whoever says to this mountain, 'Be taken up and cast into the sea,' and does not doubt in his heart, but believes that what he says will come to pass, it will be done for him. Therefore I tell you, whatever you ask in prayer, believe that you have received it, and it will be yours." (Mark 11:22-24)*

Response: As I trust in God, the seeming obstacles are removed from my path. My way is clear. In faith I speak the Truth, and God establishes my good unto me. Praise God!

Leader: *"My soul magnifies the Lord, and my spirit rejoices in God my Savior . . . he has filled the hungry with good things." (Luke 1:46, 53)*
Response: God is my all-sufficiency in all things. I feast on the living word of Truth from God, my Source. Praise God!

Leader: *"The seed is the word of God. . . . as for that in the good soil, they are those who, hearing the word, hold it fast in an honest and good heart, and bring forth fruit with patience." (Luke 8:11, 15)*
Response: The divine law of universal increase is now active in my mind and in my life. I hold steadfastly to the truth, and I reap a rich harvest of blessings. Praise God!

Leader: *Jesus said to them, "My food is to do the will of him who sent me, and to accomplish his work. Do you not say, 'There are yet four months, then comes the harvest'? I tell you, lift up your eyes, and see how the fields are already white for harvest." (John 4:34-35)*
Response: God's will for me is good and only good. I appropriate God's creative ideas, and I AM nourished and uplifted. I do not wait to give thanks, but I gratefully express God's ideas *right now* in loving and positive ways. Praise God!

Leader: *Jesus said to them, "I am the bread of life; he who comes to me shall not hunger, and he who believes in me shall never thirst." (John 6:35)*
Response: Christ is the life of my life. The Christ indwelling is the I AM—the eternal, perfect, real of me that continually renews and refreshes me. Praise God!

Leader: *And Jesus lifted up his eyes and said, "Father, I thank thee that thou hast heard me. I knew that thou hearest me always." (John 11:41-42)*
Response: I give thanks for the many blessings of life, and that I AM ever in the presence of our all-loving, all-providing Father. In the name and nature of our Way-Shower, Jesus Christ, Praise God! Amen.

Advent Blessing Responsive Prayer   5

Leader: *For this Holy feast of hope and great expectation, we let the power of our imaginations cast blessings on all the events of the days ahead. We dedicate ourselves as channels for the coming of the grace and Truth of the Christ upon the Earth. We ask God's blessings on our homes.*
Response: We invite the prospering activity of the Holy Spirit to bless our homes with warmth, order, and love.

Leader: *We ask God's special blessings for the children; for their dreams, their hopes, their joy.*

Response: We bless our children and behold in them the pure joy and beauty of Christ love.

Leader: *We ask the blessings of divine graciousness on the Christmas tree and every revered symbol of the Holy season.*

Response: Divine love graciously and lavishly supplies the beauty of Christmas.

Leader: *We ask the Spirit of guidance to aid the selection of the gifts we purchase and prepare to give.*

Response: Divine intelligence guides us in the giving and receiving of gifts. We give lovingly and receive graciously.

Leader: *We ask the Spirit of life to bless the preparation of the holiday food.*

Response: Divine love blesses the hand that prepares every sweet morsel and fills every receiver with delight and well-being.

Leader: *We ask God's presence at parties and gatherings of friends and families.*

Response: Divine love brings harmony, enjoyment, and healing love wherever two or more are gathered in His name this Holy season.

Leader: *We ask the peace of the Christ to manifest in the world this Christmas.*

Response: The Christ of peace expresses from every human heart and the Earth rejoices in the spirit of brotherhood and our Oneness with God.

Leader: *The lights of Christmas symbolize our illumined hearts. We have joined together to prepare for the coming of the Christ. We open our hearts and our minds to this reality. Let the Christ be born in us this day!*

Response: Accept our thankful hearts, O loving God.

6   Christmas Responsive Reading
(Luke 2:8-14 A.V.)

Leader: *And there were in the same country shepherds abiding in the field, keeping watch over their flock by night.*

Response: I AM a joyous shepherd. I keep careful watch over my every thought.

Leader: *And, lo, the angel of the Lord came upon them, and the glory of the Lord shone round about them: and they were sore afraid.*

Response: I AM aware of the law of my being. I stand in awe of its far-reaching magnitude in my life.

Leader: *And the angel said unto them, Fear not: for, behold, I bring you good tidings of great joy, which shall be to all people.*

Response: I AM fearless and free, for my faith in God brings good tidings of great joy to me. I share my joy with all people.

Leader:	*For unto you is born this day in the city of David a Saviour, which is Christ the Lord. And this shall be a sign unto you; Ye shall find the babe wrapped in swaddling clothes, lying in a manger.*
Response:	I AM aware that a Saviour, the Christ, is born in me this day. I welcome this Babe wrapped in swaddling clothes, lying in the manger of my heart.

Leader:	*And suddenly there was with the angel a multitude of the heavenly host praising God, and saying, Glory to God in the highest, and on earth peace, good will toward men.*
Response:	I feel the peace of my indwelling Christ child. A multitude of joy wells up within me. Glory to God in the highest! Amen.

Christmas Candlelighting Service 7

Leader:	*This candle is lit for the disciple: (repeat before each disciple)* *Peter, who represents Faith.*
Response:	My faith in the Christ presence and power within me sustains me in all that I do.

Leader:	*Andrew, who represents Strength.*
Response:	My strength is in my awareness of the Christ light within me.

Leader:	*James, the son of Zebedee, who represents Judgment.*
Response:	My judgment is keen, my choices are sound, for the Christ within me is my guide.

Leader:	*John, who represents Love.*
Response:	I AM loving, kind, patient, and totally responsive to the needs of others. I AM at all times an expressor of the love of the Christ.

Leader:	*Phillip, who represents Power.*
Response:	There is only one Power—God-Power. Through the Christ within I can accomplish anything.

Leader:	*Bartholomew, who represents Imagination.*
Response:	I image only the Christ in my mind's eye. The Christ within manifests in all its glory in my mind, body, and affairs.

Leader:	*Thomas, who represents Understanding.*
Response:	I AM understanding, compassionate, and kind. I behold the Christ in everyone.

Leader:	*Matthew, who represents Will.*
Response:	The divine will is my will. I direct my thoughts into channels that are productive and Christlike.

Leader:	*James, son of Alphaeus, who represents Order.*

Response: Through the Christ, divine order is now established in every area of my life.

Leader: *Simon, the Cananaean, who represents Zeal.*
Response: I AM filled with zeal. Through the Christ within, my enthusiasm for life and living is boundless. Praise God!

Leader: *Thaddaeus, who represents Elimination.*
Response: I eliminate from my life everything that does not contribute to my spiritual growth, and I increase in awareness of the Christ.

Leader: *Judas, who represents Life.*
Response: The life of God is my life. I live it fully, freely, and joyfully in the Christ Spirit.

8   Christmas Candlelighting Service

Affirmative Prayers for the Twelve Disciples

Leader: *I light this candle for: (repeat before each disciple)*
Peter, who represents Faith.
Response: Through the Christ faith within me, my faith is made steadfast. I hold firm, and I am courageous.

Leader: *Andrew, who represents Strength.*
Response: Through the Christ strength within me, I am made strong. I have the fortitude to overcome all things.

Leader: *James, son of Zebedee, who represents Judgment.*
Response: Through the Christ Mind within me, I make wise decisions. Divine justice is established in my life.

Leader: *John, who represents divine Love.*
Response: Through the Christ love within me, I AM now filled with peace and harmony. I attract good into my life.

Leader: *Philip, who represents spiritual Power.*
Response: Through the Christ power within me, my words go forth to accomplish God's purposes in my life.

Leader: *Bartholomew, who represents Imagination.*
Response: By the imaging power of the indwelling Christ, I now see the good in every person and every situation.

Leader: *Thomas, who represents spiritual Understanding.*
Response: Through the light of the indwelling Christ, I understand the Truth about myself. I AM a child of God, loved and worthy.

Leader: *Matthew, who represents Will.*

Response: The indwelling Christ guides my will. I let God's perfect will be done in all that I think, say, and do.

Leader: *James, son of Alphaeus, who represents divine Order.*

Response: The indwelling Christ establishes order in my life now. All things are working together for good.

Leader: *Simon, the Canaanite, who represents Zeal.*

Response: Christ is the motivating power within me. I am now filled with divine Zeal. I move toward my highest good.

Leader: *Thaddaeus, who represents Renunciation.*

Response: Through the power of the indwelling Christ, I AM cleansed and forgiven. I now let go of all un-Christlike thoughts and feelings. I make room for God's good to fill my life.

Leader: *Judas, who represents generative Life.*

Response: The indwelling Christ guides and governs the wellsprings of life within me. I AM energized, renewed, and restored.

Easter Responsive Reading I   9

Leader: *The Christ Spirit within me is the true source of wisdom and spiritual power.*

Response: Through the Christ Spirit within me, I AM resurrected into a greater consciousness of wisdom and spiritual power.

Leader: *The Christ Spirit within me is the true source of health and wholeness.*

Response: Through the Christ Spirit within me, I AM resurrected into a greater expression of health and wholeness.

Leader: *The Christ Spirit within me is the true source of all prosperity.*

Response: Through the Christ Spirit within me, I AM resurrected into a greater awareness of God's abundant substance.

Leader: *The Christ Spirit within me is my pattern for perfection and successful living.*

Response: Through the Christ Spirit within me, I AM resurrected and perfected in mind, body, and affairs. I AM made whole.

Easter Responsive Reading II   10

Leader: *The resurrecting Spirit of the Christ within me fills my mind with wisdom and understanding.*

Response: I AM illumined and my way is made clear. My success is assured.

Leader: *The resurrecting Spirit of the Christ within me quickens the healing life activity in every part of my being.*

Response: I AM whole, strong, and free, as God created me to be. I rejoice in my healing.

Leader: *The resurrecting Spirit of the Christ within me increases my awareness of infinite substance to meet my every need.*

Response: I AM enriched and prospered. An abundance of God's good fills my life and affairs.

Leader: *The resurrecting Spirit of the Christ within me fills my whole being with love.*

Response: I AM loving and I AM loved. I express love freely and fully.

11   Easter Responsive Reading III

Leader: *"I am the resurrection and the life." (John 11:25)*

Response: "He who follows me will not walk in darkness, but will have the light of life." (John 8:12)

Leader: *The Cross of Jesus is an emblem of triumph. It stands as the symbol of the supreme overcoming.*

Response: The Christ in me crosses out all error and reveals the Truth of eternal life. I deny the self that I may unite with the selfless. I give up the mortal that I may attain the immortal. I dissolve the thought of the physical body that I may realize the spiritual body.

Leader: *Now on the first day of the week Mary Magdalene came to the tomb early, while it was still dark, and saw that the stone had been taken away from the tomb. (John 20:1)*

Response: I now remove the stone of doubt from the tomb and allow the Christ within me to come forth. Christ within me is my glory! The brightness of His presence wipes out all darkness, and I AM filled with light, life, and peace.

Leader: *We shall pass over the dark hour of the cross briefly as the shadow of a hand across the light of the sun, for His message is:*

Response: I AM the resurrection and the life. I rise triumphant, splendid, glorious, and free.

12   New Beginnings—A Responsive Reading

Leader: *If any one is in Christ, he is a new creation; the old has passed away, behold, the new has come. (II Cor. 5:17)*

Response: I AM not bound by the past. I AM made new in Christ.

Leader: *This is a new day!*
Response: Through the power of the Christ in me, I see myself in a new light.

Leader: *This is a new day!*
Response: Through the power of the Christ in me, I see my strengths; I count my blessings.

Leader: *This is a new day!*
Response: Through the power of the Christ in me, I release the old; I behold the new.

Leader: *God has placed within us all that we need for full and joyous lives.*
Response: Through the power of the Christ in me, I accept my divine inheritance.

Leader: *And he who sat upon the throne said, "Behold, I make all things new." (Rev. 21:5)*
Response: This is a new day. Through the power of the Christ in me, I begin again. (Or, I begin anew.)

Blessing for a Child Responsive Reading   13

Leader: *Blessed be this child of God, whose very beginning is as our own.*
Response: May he (she) feel his (her) kinship with the Spirit of the universe and his (her) brotherhood with all mankind.

Leader: *Blessed be this child of love, who reflects the love of God.*
Response: May he (she) feel the love others give to him (her), the love he (she) gives to others, and come to know there is but one love—God.

Leader: *Blessed be this child of life, whose very being stems from the action of God.*
Response: May life always flow easily within him (her) and may he (she) increase the movement of God within others.

Leader: *Blessed be this child of wisdom, whose ever-expanding mind will touch the fount of knowing.*
Response: May he (she) learn to listen to the words and feelings of others, and to the voice of God in prayer, for through these come understanding.

Leader: *Blessed be this child of eternity, who has no Alpha and no Omega.*
Response: May the path he (she) walks always lead him (her) to the highest pinnacles of life, love, and wisdom; and may he (she) guide others by the life he (she) lives.

All: Thank You, Father, for another expression of Your eternal, loving presence.

Scripture: "And he took bread, and when he had given thanks he broke it and gave it to them, saying, 'This is my body which is given for you. Do this in remembrance of me.' And likewise the cup after supper, saying, 'This cup which is poured out for you is the new covenant in my blood.' " (Luke 22:19-20)

Introduction: This part of the Scriptures symbolizes the Word and the Twelve Powers of the soul. This means a great deal when you realize that you are the Word feeding the spiritual powers of your soul with spoken words of Truth. The cup, from which the powers of the soul are to drink, is the participation in the activities of life to the fullest. Bread represents the spoken word of Truth. Wine represents life and its activities.

As we join in this responsive reading, we are appropriating these words of Truth.

Faith (Peter)

Leader: *"I will give you the keys of the kingdom." (Matt. 16:19)*
Response: I have faith in God. I have faith in Spirit. I have faith in the Invisible.

Strength (Andrew)

Leader: *"He who endures to the end will be saved." (Mark 13:13)*
Response: I am strong in the Lord and in the power of His might.

Judgment (James)

Leader: *"The Father judges no one, but has given all judgment to the Son."*
            (John 5:22)
Response: I have faith in God's wisdom to guide me in expressing good judgment.

Love (John)

Leader: *"You shall love the Lord your God with all your heart, and with all your soul, and with all your mind." (Matt. 22:37)*
Response: I have faith in the power of God's love. It equalizes and harmonizes mind, body, and affairs.

Power (Phillip)

Leader: *"You will decide on a matter, and it will be established for you." (Job 22:28)*
            "All authority in heaven and on earth has been given to me." (Matt. 28:18)
Response: I have faith in God's power of the spoken word to lift me out of darkness into light.

Imagination (Bartholomew)

Leader: *"You shall see greater things than these. . . . you will see heaven opened, and the angels of God ascending and descending upon the Son of man." (John 1:50, 51)*

Response: My imagination is constructive. It is filled with positive pictures of good. Thank You, Father.

Will (Matthew)

Leader: *"Not every one who says to me, 'Lord, Lord,' shall enter the kingdom of heaven, but he who does the will of my Father who is in heaven." (Matt. 7:21)*

Response: I realize that there is only one will—God's good will.

Understanding (Thomas)

Leader: *"I am the way, and the truth, and the life; no one comes to the Father but by me." (John 14:6)*

Response: Through the spoken word, I AM raised to a higher understanding of all life.

Divine Order (James the less)

Leader: *"In everything God works for good with those who love him." (Rom. 8:28)*

Response: I am established in divine order, and I daily adjust to the new things that are working in and through my life.

Zeal (Simon)

Leader: *"The servant is not greater than his lord." (John 13:16 A.V.)*

Response: God is my vitality and energy. My zeal is spiritually guided.

Renunciation/Denial (Thaddaeus)

Leader: *"Let what you say be simply 'Yes' or 'No'; anything more than this comes from evil." (Matt. 5:37)*

Response: I deny error as soon as I AM aware of it. I release, loose, and let go, and let God.

Life (Judas)

Leader: *"I am the resurrection and the life; he who believes in me, though he die, yet shall he live." (John 11:25)*

Response: I am alive, alert, awake, joyous, and enthusiastic about life; and I go forth to meet my good.

TOPICAL INDEX

ADVENT and CHRISTMAS
Nos. 259-274, 276-291

THE CHRIST
Nos. 58-65

CONSECRATION
Nos. 241-247, 251-258
Let, 92
Purer in Heart, O God, 235
Take My Life and Let It Be, 236
The Bread That Giveth Strength, 169
Truth Will Lift Me, 238
With a Perfect Heart, 249

EASTER and SPRING
Nos. 292-298
Christ the Lord Is Risen Today, 300
Lord of the Dance, 301

FAITH
Nos. 156-165
Only Believe, 152
The Chant of the Ongoers, 240

GUIDANCE and ILLUMINATION
Nos. 109-118, 120-129
God's Holy Presence Is in Me, 136
Holy Spirit, Truth Divine, 94, 95
I Clothe Myself Safely Round, 66
I Lift Mine Eyes unto the Hills, 51
Oh, Fill Me with Thy Presence, Lord, 40
Open My Eyes, That I May See, 72
Perfection, 47
Sing the Glorious Words, 191
Sweep Over My Soul, 145
The Love in Me, 177
The Power to Heal, 133
The Prayer of Faith, 78, 79
'Tis the Gift to Be Simple, 338

HEALING
Nos. 130-139
Amazing Grace, 16
Eternal Life in Me, 302
Living Abundantly, 111

JOY SONGS and SUNDAY SCHOOL SONGS
Nos. 314-359
As We're Sowing, 307
Festival of Life, 193
God Is Good, 176

I Am God's Melody of Life, 186
I Am the Image of God, 184
I Am the Radiant Life of God, 183
I'm Alive, 187
I'm One with God, 194
I'm the Expression of Infinite Life, 185
I Live in the Kingdom of Light, 50
Kum Ba Yah, 98
Let's Celebrate Life, 192
Love Is the Answer, 122
Love Is the Only Power, 119
Quietly, 105
Thank You, Father, 311
The Gospel in One Word Is Love, 237
Walking Is a Prayer, 250
Work Wonders from Within, 125

LIFE
Nos. 180-188
Festival of Life, 193
Let's Celebrate Life, 192
Life Is for Living, 195
Wonderful Words of Life, 190

LOVE
Nos. 167-173, 175-179
God Is Love, 165
Love Is the Answer, 122
Love Is the Only Power, 119
Saviour, Teach Me, Day by Day, 87

MORNING and EVENING
A Morning Song, 189
Abide with Me, 102
All Praise to Thee, My God, 99, 100
Day Is Dying in the West, 107
Heavenly Father, Grant Thy Blessing, 67
Holy, Holy, Holy, Lord God Almighty, 4
Morning Has Broken, 6
Now the Day Is Over, 104
Vesper Hymn, 202

NEW BEGINNINGS and CHANGING SEASONS
Nos. 220-234
Oh! That Is Now Glory for Me, 11
The Morn of Truth Is Breaking, 23, 24

OMNIPRESENCE
Nos. 38-42, 44-52, 54-57
All Hail the Power, 13
God of the Earth, the Sky, the Sea, 9

TOPICAL INDEX

INDEX OF TUNE NAMES

INDEX OF TUNE NAMES

INDEX OF TUNE NAMES

INDEX OF TITLES AND FIRST LINES

INDEX OF TITLES AND FIRST LINES

INDEX OF TITLES AND FIRST LINES

INDEX OF TITLES AND FIRST LINES

INDEX OF TITLES AND FIRST LINES

INDEX OF TITLES AND FIRST LINES

SELECTED READINGS

RESPONSIVE READINGS

RESPONSIVE READINGS

Printed U.S.A.
29-S-5698-50M-4-84